# Roamer of planes

D1784957

# Roamer of planes
# (Former title: My life)

## Steve Taylor

Original title:
Steve Taylor / *Létsíkok vándora*
novum pro Kiadó, 2009


Translated by:
Salacz Veronika
2010


Cover design by
Salacz Veronika




First edition




ISBN 9781463672232

I recommend this book to my friends and my enemies who don't even guess how much I learn from them. Thanks for everyone, with whom I had any kind of relationship, which lead me to get this book accomplished. My special, utmost thanks go to my wife and my children, who left me enough time willy–nilly to write this book. I tell them and everyone else: We all know how our road ends, but the goal is not the essence in it, only the road and the experiences we gather throughout this time.

# First Chapter

I was born somewhere in Eastern Europe 35 years ago. In the Calvinist christening I got the name Steve Taylor. My bringing–up in communistic mentality, resulted me having an atheist view of life. My father worked as a carpenter, my mother as an administrator. My childhood was fairly diverse. I often thought a lot about great matters of life, such as life and death. I might have been about seven years old when I was having a bath one night and I started to cry, because I was wondering about what was going to happen if one of my parents would die and never tell me again "Come here my son, hug me and give me a kiss!"

Who is going to tell me: "Good boy, you are clever"? I was crying very loud. First my mother then my father came into the bathroom, and asked me:

– My son, what happened to you? What is the problem?

But I was just standing in the bathtub and sobbing. I struggled against the tears streaming from my eyes with my two little fists, with not much success. They managed to calm me down only after a long time. Every night for a whole week, in the bathtub I was weeping, but only quietly.

Now I know that it was not useless, but somebody could have told me!

Do you change clothes? How often a day? How do you do this? Slowly or quickly? Do you remember what were you wearing after you took it off? Do you know beforehand what you put on or do you just choose it by guess? Imagine that death is only a changing of clothes: you put on some other clothes somewhere else, and keep on living. You can ask "how"? Well, I suggest that everyone should choose the one which is the best according to his or her abilities and the information that he or she possess!

I might have been 16 years old, when one afternoon I was lying on my back in the bed. I was alone in the house; I turned my head a bit aside to let my tongue block my throat. I started breathing in turns, through my left and right nostril. I put together my two feet, and crossed my arms on my chest. I started to slow down my respiration, and at the same time I let all my thoughts go except one.

– I want to fly! – I kept on saying the same to myself without thinking on any specific method to do this.

I did not rise from the bed, but I didn't even want to.

Whereas, something absolutely different, unexpected thing happened!

I was not thinking of anything, I was lying there motionless. Suddenly I felt like something opens at the middle of my skull, and slowly great warmth was overflowing me till my toes. My body was in heat, like it was pure lava flowing from a volcano. I became very hot, then I suddenly sat up. I looked back on the bed and saw myself lying on the bed from torso and down. And I saw something else: a brightly shinning silver cord was attaching me to my real body.

I could stare at this only for a few seconds, since a voice that existed merely in my mind warned me that I have to turn back. However, in the next moment something else happened as well…

– I am here. Did you want to fly? Come with me!

I was very surprised, as I realised my first visitor of the astral world wearing a black wide–brimmed hat and a black poncho. We started to communicate, but it was not really reassuring: I was afraid from his figure vibrating in black. Suddenly, I gave away to weakness; I had to put my hands involuntarily over my mouth. I slightly leant forward, and all my teeth fell into my palms… or at least according to my feelings.

Both of my bodies started to shake. An undetermined weakness, nausea, sickish feeling overwhelmed me. My first thought was this: loss of power! My teeth fell out! They are also parts of my bones. The frame weakened!

– I won't go with you now. Thank you for the possibility. For me this is the first time. I will find you later – I replied, concentrating very hard on this thought.

– All right, as you wish. I will wait for you. See you next time! – and he disappeared.

Since then we have become close, good friends. He became one of the determinant members of the family from my other world. I like him, as the others as well.

However, after the first visiting I retired to myself, and to my body lying on the bed, and slowly sat up. I remembered everything. A form of unspeakable terror took over me.

I might have been about to die, or what was this?

Now I sat up with my whole self, and reached into my mouth with both hands. I was searching for my teeth, could find all of them. Until today I have them all, and they are stronger than ever.

I'm grateful for the trees of the forest, which I choose during my long bike tours. These are sympathetic trees for me, and according to my feelings they give me a huge amount of energy. I take a walk to them, while hugging them I concentrate on energy transfer: I get it from the earth through them. From the beloved, ancient Mother Earth, who is the base of everything.

While riding on the bicycle I feel the power of the wind. The air imbibes me, fills all my cells up with energy. As I'm passing by, I feel the sweet breeze kissing me.

Arriving to a lake, stream, or standing in the rain, I feel the power of the water as it pierces through everything – and slowly it smashes gigantic mountains to tiny little stones.

But I could think of the fire, when staring at the fireplace I see the flames, and I feel as they warm me up and purify me from all illnesses and damaging thoughts.

But aether is the base of any other cosmic element. The focused slowed down breathing, that I practised wittingly and unwittingly before, resulted that first I didn't feel inhaling – actually I was not breathing in a physical sense.

The aether is what we are from as well. And after we passed through all the five elements, expending enough time on all of them, maybe our days can pass more calmly. All this can help a lot in the solution of our life problems. And for sure, we shouldn't forget to listen to music either, since it is suitable for many things. According to latest research, classical music is very soothing for babies, while other music waves are able to bring the feeling or the pseudo–feeling of togetherness for people, who are under the effects of drugs or alcohol or "only" suffering from inferiority complex, distress, lack of praise, and who try to be happy under these moments. Although, they are hardly aware that in the meantime they release enormous conscious energies. Namely, this vast amount of joy–searching, stress reducing self–forgotten dance is capable of freeing great inner energies. This effect especially catches the newly arrived ones, who firstly observe only unwittingly that they felt good. They experience the whole situation pleasant, which can be increased by the effects of drugs. For instance, marketing presentations held for many people, from any kind of product, can work perfectly based on this mass behaviour.

But how exactly does this work? Well, a business man, who seems to be successful, makes a presentation and explains with the help of witnesses that his method is the only one which will help us to solve our financial and other problems, and only the money earned by the help of his system can make us a happy, family–loving person with a lot of free time – so all our aims, dreams could come true.

# Second Chapter

Many people want to buy a new car, something sporty and perhaps fast.

Some people have these vehicles, but they can't take advantage of them, simply because there's no place to drive them. Although, they can tell their friends that they have it provoking their tribute in this way.

I was 18 years old when I got the driving licence for automobile and truck. I have never wanted to get is for motorcycle...

I was supposedly fifteen years old when on a summer morning, the school was already over, there was a middle–aged woman ringing the door, of our house with a garden. She explained to my mother that my father, who always went to work with his motorcycle in those times, which was about twenty kilometres away, was hit by a bus in front of the woman's house. Father flew ten metres into the bushes at the side of the road. At that time there were no cell phones. The lady got to know our address from the ambulance men, who managed to cut the leather jacket off my father, in which they found his identity card with his address. We went to the site of the accident. The broken motorcycle was there; it was bumped by a bus. It was the bus drivers fault; he didn't give the priority on the road to my father. He never got the proper punishment, compared to the fact that he was driving drunk already in the early morning.

Next time I saw my father was in the afternoon, lying on his back in the hospital. It was the crash helmet that saved his life. The long green streak of bark on the top of the helmet showed that this is where he met the roadside tree. A fair–sized piece of skin was cut out from his shin, and was put this on his left thigh, because due to the injury he suffered, his muscles could be seen. Nothing happened to his head, the helmet protected it. He was in the hospital for more than eight months, because of different internal lesions.

These months awfully wore out our family. My younger brother cried a lot, I had to console him. My mother went to visit my father almost every day after work, when she came home sometimes she was happier, sometimes sadder. We always asked about our father. In the first few months she was quite down–hearted as well.

I was 20 years old when under the selective military service I passed the driving test for bus and container lorry (alias truck) as well. I knew, later on I will need them.

The day of my driving test for the car was Friday. There were ten of us on the practical examination. According to the list of names, I was the last one. As I sat into the car, first I adjusted the seat, then the mirrors. I got the order of practices for obligatory parking lots. I solved these tasks slowly and perfectly. Then we left the test routes, and drove into traffic. After a short time the inspector told me that his weekend house was close, and he was about to build a house on it, therefore he needed some cement, so we go to the closest building material lot and check the prices. He knew that I was going to do the practical driving test for the truck in the afternoon. We arrived to the lot and he found cement for a good price. When he sat back into the car he told me that I passed the driving test for car and now we were going to get the bigger car on which we will carry the material to his house, and if all of this happens, everything will be fine. And so it was.

I was enrolled for bus at the army as well. Beforehand I had to pass a psychological aptitude test. Doing it for the first time, I drove half of the bus at the side of the road. At that time we had an elderly, bearded driving instructor who was shouting at me for about 15 minutes then he told me to swap places with one of my soldier mates because he was not able to stand my style. For me the position of the driver's place was determining, because in the truck, the half–way line was about one metre from the place where I sat, but in the bus it was only thirty–forty centimetres. With the difference of these two numbers was the bus hanging down the roadside. Unfortunately, I managed to sweep some smaller branches at the side of the road. My instructor feared the rear view mirror very much, and he drew my attention to this fact with a high–power roar. Two weeks later a high ranked officer, who had to check the level of the education that day, travelled with us.

Coming out from the military base, I sat at the steering wheel of the bus. I was aware of everything. I drove calmly and slowly, opened out the throttle carefully, followed at a safe distance, I braked easy and circumspectly. As the officer saw how I drove, he said the following:

– When you drive, you always have to be aware of the movements and behaviour of other people in traffic, and for the vehicle signs driven by them. You have to pick out the intractable, and have to be as far from them as possible during traffic. You have to pay attention to dogs and cats, not running over them, imaging them as future wall carpets.

I accepted his orders, later on they came to my advantage.

I only had three hours to drive container lorry before the exam, but it was enough for me, I did not need more time.

I had the practical exams for bus and truck on the same day.

It was on a slightly cold November morning. However, we didn't have to wear too many clothes since fortunately on the old bus, which we drove, the heating worked well. I was the fourth examiner. Before me, my three soldier mates passed the exam. I got a quite risky route; I had to drive on a road which was parallel with the suburb railway in one of the outer district of the city. On one side of the road there were cars parking half of it on the road, other half on the pavement. On the other side, there was a traffic island extending, where passengers getting out of the train step on. I was driving at this part when suddenly a Mini Morris arrived next to me.

It was a small car, so we hardly had enough space on the road next to each other. As we went on, some cars were parked in a way on the road, which seemed to be wide enough at first for me and the Mini, but it became tighter and tighter. I looked down from the driver's seat and saw a middle–aged woman, who looked at me frightened and was gesticulating with her hands towards me. I guess she was afraid that she, or her husband sitting next to her, is going to cause a problem. Realizing the situation, my examiner broke out into a terrific roar.

– What does this car driver next to us want? How could she wriggle herself next to us? Didn't she see that this is a learner bus driver? – Then he leaned closer to the window over the steering wheel, and said calmly to me:

– All right, young man. Leave the other vehicle to get in front of you, then keep a reasonable following distance.

– The great mother of these ones! – He continued – Can't she see from her own eyes? She must have got her licence by credit. Always so many problems with these car drivers! My son, you passed the exam – he told me, calmly turned to me.

My instructor, after we stopped and talked in private, rowed me, because of me getting into this situation, and not caring about it. While he was talking, I was calmly smiling into his face. I didn't say a word, I was glad that I managed to pass the practical exam for bus, and was already waiting for my second exam in the afternoon for container–lorry. After a few hours it was my turn. We went towards the truck cabin, me, my instructor and my inspector. The two trainers had a short conversation without me. After I sat in, only the inspector who tested me for the bus got in the truck.

– Young man, you slowly roll out from the parking lot, we go to the main square, do a circle to our right, and you park back here. If everything is okay, you will pass. We will have three traffic lights on our way – he said.

I did the road, paying attention to all the small details. However, I entered the parking area with too big speed. I stepped on the brake with full power, that's how I stopped. I shut off the engine, and looked at the man sitting next to me, who had a wide smile on his face:

– All right, soldier; you fulfilled the task – he acknowledged.

I got out from the cabin; I was happy, but was going towards my instructor with a poker face, who was already shouting at me from a long distance:

– I knew you would fail, I knew it!

He wore a malicious smile. I waited until I got close enough to him. Perhaps one meter from him I replied, so that the others could hear me as well:

– Unfortunately, I passed this exam as well, I'm sorry, with best respect, and thank you for everything.

Hearing this, my mates broke out into a loud laugh, which lasted for minutes. It was a cheerful, hearty laugh coming from deep inside. Music to my ears!

# Third Chapter

A familiar voice spoke to me from inside.

– Are you writing this book? It is enough for today! It's too late. There would be something for you to do. You also have some work in the material world, as well as here, you know. Come, we have to talk about some things regarding to your further life. Yin and Yang – The former is your material life; the latter is your astral one. I know that you like both of them that's why we are waiting for you.

– Fine, 10 pm. I'm going to work tomorrow as well. Although, according to this, I'm going far away at night, I'm going to be with highly educated, fastidious, good old friends, which is always a pleasure to me. It's even better that we can't meet in the material world. We live in all corners of the world. On the astral plane it's easier: you don't need a flight ticket, you don't need to book anything, there's no train, no luggage, only me in a light sphere. If I go far away, I just need to unravel from it.

Involuntarily, I put on my best astral body. I move fresh and youthfully in the aether, as fast as possible. Moon – Earth, two hours there and back. Not bad, is it? It's fortunate that I also learned it, like riding a bicycle. Nowadays it works well. Or at least I think it does, but of course everything is relative. You are going to learn it as well, but you'll have a few thousand steps of purification in your mind. Slowly you are going to build up your own small, inner spacecraft, and you will reach your goals, which all of your inner parts want to achieve, with the speed thousand times faster than the thought, no matter how far they are.

When we are small children, and have never seen a bicycle, we don't know anything about its existence, neither how to use it. If we see the first person riding a bike, maybe we start to think what is the old man on the bicycle doing? Then we get our first bike. First we need help to set off, but after a while our parents realise that we don't need help anymore, we can ride safely, independently. Later on they let us go alone; first only for short distances, but later on further and further. We grow up and manoeuvre very well. Some of us hold the handlebar with only one hand; others don't even hold it just balance on the bike, and ride it wherever they want to. Some do everything on an artistic level with their beloved cycles: they hop, jump or turn in the air as much as they want to.

How do you use your conscious and unconsciousness? And your body? Like a professional cyclist? Do you want to learn? Or you are interested in something else that you are able to do?

# Fourth Chapter

After primary school, which lasted for eight years, I studied to be a carpenter. After that next to having a job, I graduated in a night school, which lasted for three years. At my first workplace, in a huge factory, I had to repair substandard leaf doors which were damaged in the course of quantity production. Practically I worked at the final phase of all works with an elderly colleague, who was retired. I got a lot of help from him. His favourite quote was: Don't bother with anyone! Whatever they say only one thing is sure. If you work, do it nicer, better and faster than any of your colleagues. Don't wait for your boss to praise your work because it is rather rare. If you are known by your colleagues, and your contracting parties, then your boss will praise you consequently as well. I do it like this, my son. I have already been here for 32 years, and I have never heard that I'm going to be fired. I'll leave if I get bored, but the problem would be that then I'd be bored at home.

He was always a happy fellow. He was small, and had a slightly bent back. Every morning he arrived to the workplace freshly shaved, in clean clothes, and ironed shirt. He respected himself. After changing clothes and having the usual morning appointment, we went to work. During work, I paid attention to his movements. After a while I discovered that he doesn't do any unnecessary movements.

One day a family of coloured skin moved into our neighbourhood. You could hear some racist remarks in the street, but after a while it turned out that the members of the family are very friendly. The name of the head of the family was Karel, his wife was Rita, and they had only one child, David. After they got to know what my job was, they asked me for some smaller repairs in their house. All of these works were easy: fixing chairs, hinge setting etc.

In half a year, we visited them a few nights for a grill party or a dinner. We became quite good friends. At weekends they saw me several times leaving with my race bicycle for short tours, and coming back only after a few hours. Usually I rode the bike for 30–50 kilometres depending on the weather and my fitness. On my ways sometimes I also went to nature conservation areas through narrower forest paths, where I saw hares running as well as stags and deers. Once I was so lucky that I could glimpse a boar; it was alone in the middle of the oak forest crunching the fruits of the trees with its teeth. Its big white tusks where shinning from very far. This was what I realised first; as I looked in the direction of the oak forest, and glimpsed something white moving up and down in a methodical rhythm. I realised only later, after I sneaked closer, what it actually was. It was eating in its own utter calmness; seemingly it enjoyed the food.

One summer my father brought home a three month old grey, mixed–breed puppy. His parents were a Giant Schnauzer and a German shepherd. When he was one year old, he was already full–grown. His favourite game was spinning a middle–sized pebble with both his front feet on the pavement in front of the house. After that, he turned his head a bit aside, opened his mouth, approached the pebble, and tried to pick it up with his mouth. Sometimes it worked out, sometimes it didn't. I saw his game several times. Later on I looked for bigger and bigger stones, and by the age of two he was running around with stones as big as my fist. He could pick these up easier with his mouth. I could see the effect of his hobby on his body as well; his neck became wider than his head. All the collars were coming down from his neck; we had to buy a halter for him.

I got an iron ball from someone. Its diameter was around eight centimetres. First Felix, my dog, didn't even pay attention to it. Then I rolled it away for him. He picked up on its noise as it was rolling on the concrete, then he ran after it and rolled it with his legs. Its methodical movement pleased him; he came to like it very much. It could be also known from other signs such as, during nights big thuds could be heard as he let the ball fall down from his mouth onto the concrete, and then the noise of the rolling as the iron was trundling on the concrete. Then a small pause and the thudding again. The result of his "easy voluntary workout" was that by the age of three, we had to shift his halter five centimetres bigger. Since I took him plenty times for a walk with a collar alongside the bike, he knew the area. At the nature reservations he gave a chase to the hares several times, but he never caught any of them, because even though he was getting near them more quickly, the chased hare always took a perfect ninety degree turn, sometimes left, sometimes right. By the time Felix realised the change of direction, he had already ran five or six metres, then stopped. Noticing that there was no prey in front of him, he looked around, and while catching a sight of it, he ran after it again. The chases usually ended at the entrances of hilly rabbit holes, where the preys fled from the chase.

After some sniffing and scrapping, the dog, hearing me call him, came back to me, and as a reward I always petted his head. These times his eyes were full of gratefulness when he looked at me. After a small amount of training he sat and laid down at command. He came next to my bike persistently, while keeping the one and a half meter distance with the collar. Usually, after we arrived home, I gave him delicious, tasty dog food as a reward, which he gobbled up immediately.

– If you work, then work! If you eat, then eat! If you sleep, then sleep! Do always in your mind what your body does, because then everything is going to be fine! Pay attention to the maximum!

Felix became a very good friend of mine. When we met in the morning, and in the afternoon, he always sidled to me, while wagging his tail. I didn't really have to talk to him much, after a while I realised that if I think of him strongly, with love, and I ask him in this way to do something, he does it. By the age of four I didn't talk to him anymore. Now that I recall this, it is a bit strange. It was unnecessary to shout his name when he ran after a hare on the field. This was the first time. Then I realised, telepathy based on love can exist between a human and an animal as well. I called him back by only thinking of him. He was two hundred metres away from me. He stopped, looked at me, then started running straight to me. As he arrived to me, he took the end of his one and a half meter long collar into his mouth, sat down, and pushed his mouth to my hands. He was waiting for me to take the collar, and after putting it on the handlebar, continuing our way.

Sometimes I stopped with him at a stream or a smaller lake to have a rest for a few minutes, then drank a bit. On summers, when it was very hot, he jumped into the water, and took a long swim. We didn't rush each other, sometimes he needed a few a minutes to rest, sometimes I stopped. By that time I hadn't been talking to him in a human voice for a year. One summer morning, after stepping out of the house, I didn't hear his voice running towards me. I started to search, where could he be. When I found him I thought he was sleeping. It was strange that he didn't wake up to my approach either. I went to him, and petted him. Something suggested that he was not living here anymore. I started to cry, and I wished I could just meet him somewhere! I carried him to the back of our garden, and dug a grave. I buried him. I said a small pray for him, then I went to work. That day work didn't go so well. By the question of my old colleague, I told him what happened.

– It was only a dog – he said.

– No, it was not only a dog, he was much more – I replied.

– Well, you know if it would have been one of your relatives, sorry for putting it this way, I don't want to hurt you, but then I would understand that it stirs you up so much. But try to work as usual! You have work for today, and for tomorrow as well, pay attention and do them – he said.

Work was going roughly, but after a few hours I relaxed – for some reason I felt that I was going to see him again, I just didn't know when and where.

After shift I went home, did what I had to, then at night before going to bed, I don't know why, but I cleaned of everything from the other bed standing next to mine. It became absolutely free. The two beds formed an L shape.

I laid down on my back as usual, and pulled the blanket on myself. I started my everyday pray. I beseech Thee, my Lord that all living beings should be imbibed by the vital energy, let them be in any world, from the smallest to the biggest one. Let us love our enemies also, since they teach us something as well. What they do, is a good aim for them, merely the consequences of their acts may be bad for us. Help them and us too. Let the energy of love imbibe everything in this cosmic world; let the vital energy flow, wherever living beings and matters exist. The ancient vibration in me can be found in everything and everywhere, thus I am in everything everywhere as well. I'M IN EVERYTHING EVERYWHERE! I love all parts of my body I use, because it listens to me, and does things for the improvement of my conscious and body. For the prosperity of other living beings, for them rising to higher planes, I would like to listen to all the wishes my body asks from me. Thus I have to move my body, and in the meantime pay attention to it, and make it do exercises, keep it busy, rest it, feed it. That ancient God, which created us, takes care about us, and gives us what we need. Thank you and I really wish that the energy and the vibration of the Universe reaches the soul of my deceased dog, and raise HIM to a higher level in the circulation of rebirth. Thank you, my God, for this day. Give a peaceful dream to me and for everyone tonight. For tomorrow I wish all living creatures, wherever they are, a calm day. For all creatures without a body, all souls, who are waiting to get a material body again, and to be born somewhere to learn according to his improvement level, by reaching a higher level in the world. Good night to everyone.

I raised my hands upwards, perpendicularly upwards, with open palms towards the sky. I was still lying on my back in the bed. I opened my eyes. It was completely dark in the room. I let down the shades in a way that the street lamps light couldn't get into the room. There was no light filtering in through the door either.

I was in a completely dark room then, but I love darkness. A lot of acquaintances can show up this time. Looking at my arms, I saw strange colours running from my elbows upwards and downwards. Blue, green, red, dazzling gold and their combinations. I admired my arms in turns – as if I'd have an own night–time firework around my arms. It was an interesting cavalcade of colours that I had never seen before. I was amazed by the multi–colours, and the pulsating glinting of them. It was a magnificent experience.

Then suddenly, coming from the colours above my face, another face appeared and came closer and closer to me. First I saw only the outline of it, but as it was coming closer the features became clearly visible. It was a smiley, friendly face, which, according to my feelings, beamed positive thoughts. It was floating about thirty centimetres above my head. Then I saw clearly the nose, the mouth and all small details of the face. It approached smiling, calmly, I thought him to be a friend coming from the astral world towards me. I was honoured by his visit – I thought, and even said it out loudly.

– I don't know who you are, but I'm happy you are here. I don't know why you came. I hope you are a friend, at least I think you are.

– What do you say?

He came closer to my face, maybe five centimetres. The face was put together in white, yellowish–white, and golden lights.

– I'm glad for you. We have already known you for a long time. Anyway, you have met me before, then you were very frightened. You know, I'm the black man, who wanted to take you away. For tonight I have a small surprise for you. Sleep and you are going to have an interesting dream by morning, I'm sure you will remember it. I welcome you among us. We have been looking for you for a long time, although till now you haven't been ready for the meeting. You have to learn a lot, although you won't need all your abilities here, in this world. But elsewhere you do, therefore always be very strong spiritually, believe in yourself and in others. There is no failure, only feedback. If you don't manage to do something, try it again in another way. If one way doesn't work, there will be another. I wish you a very good night.

That was his last thought. After that he shrank into a tiny white sphere, and started to go upwards very fast, then disappeared. I was very surprised by this whole thing; I was very tired as well. I turned to my right in the bed; usually I fall asleep this way: I turn on my right or left side to be in a foetus position. After this I gradually slow down my breathing. At this time you can observe very well, through which nostril does our body circulate the air. With a little help you can discover it yourself, if you push one of your nostrils in with one of your fingers to the nasal bone. You can feel the difference.

There are differences in quality, between the procedures of breathing through your left or right nostril. The left one is cool, calm, passive, and has a feminine character, while the right one is hot, stimulating, active and has a masculine character. The character of the two types of breathing comes from the movement of the orbs. During breathing normally our body switches from one nostril to the other in every one and a half hour. Paying attention to our breathing from this point of view, a smaller flu can be tided over easily. But of course it can be very useful to think it over; why don't we pay attention to the illnesses of our body and soul, and why don't we care about them. Later on they can emerge as acute sicknesses to show us our actual problems in our life. We can't run away from ourselves, but in fellowship, and with love towards ourselves we can solve the tasks with great efficiency.

In my last alert moment I remembered the last thought of my friend: – You are going to dream something memorable!

I got up, I thought. But no! I woke up only in an astral way, and sat at the side of my bed. I looked back, and saw the light of my silver cord. Although, my room was in complete darkness, I saw everything in daylight. Suddenly on the empty bed, which was next to mine, great brightness evolved for a moment. Impulsively I raised my arms in front of my eyes, but it was unnecessary, I could see through them. I was extraordinary happy; my dog, believed to be dead, lay there. I was extremely happy to see and talk to him again.

– How are you? – I asked

– Not good. What had to come came. I don't know what kind of world comes after this for me. I know you prayed a lot for me to be reborn on a higher plane; I can't be a dog again. I fear the unknown, and feel very weak. I don't know where I'm going now, where I'm going to be born to live the material life again. I know this is what is waiting for me.

– I don't know anything either – I replied. – It's good that you are here. I suppose we have to wait.

I raised my head. I could see very far. Three orange dots were coming towards us with the speed of light. As the distance became smaller between us, their conversation became more and more distinct.

– We must hurry up, we don't have much time – said the one on the left side.

The one in the middle asked:

– What is his task going to be as a human?

The third replied:

– He will take over a very important task from someone, we can be happy that he lived under good circumstances, and has learned enough for his next life.

They were coming closer extremely fast.

– I welcome you, glad we met. We haven't seen you for a long time. Now, you are going to see something you have never experienced before. Pay attention! – said the fellow on the left as he arrived. All three of them were Tibetan monks.

They surrounded my dog from three sides. They stretched their arms towards him, and prayed continuously for his rebirth. They sent golden energy beams towards the dog, till a golden bubble evolved, which totally surrounded him. In the meantime they murmured different prays, but always about the same thing. I didn't even know which one of them I should pay attention to. After a few hours they finished. Then one of them turned to me:

– If he wakes up, comfort him – he asked me. You surely will find his visible figure strange, but remember: you know his soul. Talk to that, and to his body. He will listen to you because he knows you. What is going to happen after this might be new to you, but it is natural. Everything is going to be all right. We will not come back. We wish you all the best – they said.

They quickly transformed into three tiny golden spheres, and rapidly departed. Didn't matter how much I was rubbing my eyes, if I had seen it well; I had to realise that my fist was in the place of my brain, because I was rummaging in my astral body instead of my eyes. I realised that in this world the earthly gestures, immateriality, and the effects of overlapping spaces of the parts of the astral body are absolutely different. I'm somewhere else.

As I looked at my bed, I saw a homeless person in rags with a big beard, long, sloppy hair in an alcoholic state for sure. He didn't know anything about himself. I was viewing the figure than started to talk to him involuntarily.

– You are reborn. You got this figure which is quite unusual for you right now, for now you can hardly move your limbs. You need some time until you get to learn how to use this body. You know, beforehand you lived in a body of a dog. I know your soul. I was beside you the whole time. It's magnificent that all this happened. I'm happy to be with you – I would have said, but he interrupted me.

– All right, I understood. I saw some drunken people. It is like I just started to get sober after a great drinking. How could I know what kind of feeling this is? I do, since I will feel it later on. I thank you for everything, especially that you didn't treat me like a dog, but as a friend. These are my last words. I suppose I have to go now.

I was still sitting on my bed, but I had to wake up consciously as well. I got into my slippers, and went to the switch. I turned on the light. I looked at the two beds. On mine was my blanket tossed aside a bit, and my pillow. On the other bed there were the clothes I took off yesterday. My heart was beating heavily. I was looking for something, but I didn't know what. All the small details were enacted in me again. I was staring at the beds with bulging eyes, but there was nothing that could remind me of what happened, merely my astral and my real mind knew it. I couldn't understand even after days went by, why my unconscious mind let my conscious mind get to know the story of that night.

Are other human beings able to live a night like this and a conscious day life in the same way? When is the threshold cleared? Maybe this is what protects us from negative experiences? Or is it even more than this? How many more worlds do exist that we don't know of? How can I get to these? What do I have to do with my earthly mind to be able to get there mentally? How fast can I accomplish this road? Do I need any protection? Will I or can I have fellow–passengers? What is their mentality? Are they creatures from other worlds? Are they enemies or friends? Do I have to send something or someone beforehand, so that any kind of communication can be established?

These kinds of thoughts kept my mind occupied for months, and the fact that I saw a rebirth! I was searching everywhere, I was seeking all that or who could help me to understand these things.

# Fifth Chapter

I might have been twenty years old, when I found one of my favourite books in a bookshop. The writer asks at the beginning:

– Who is driving the bus? It's your bus. Where are you sitting? Somewhere in the back or in the front, at the driver's seat? Who is driving your bus if not you? When will you be able to sit in the front? Will you have enough experience to do it? When will your moment come?

At the end of the book there was an address without a phone number, where you could write if you needed any more information, or – saying it in a modern way – wanted to take part in a personality developing course. I sent a letter, they replied.

As I arrived to the first, two day long introductory lessons, I had to realise that I was the youngest.

Eleven people came. We were quite diverse according to our professions. Among us was a psychologist, cab–driver, language teacher, lawyer, etc.

Our teacher learned, and got authorization to this educational form from the person who discovered, and found out this system.

There were some laws we had to accept as preconditions.

The behaviour of the human is determined by the idea he created about reality, and not from the real world, but the subjective. The reality of someone can change with the enlargement of his idea.

Everyone works perfectly. Nobody is guilty; it just happens that there are some people who do harmful or absolutely unnecessary things. If we do realise, how they are doing it, we may make their behaviour useful, or we can change their attitude.

A person is not equal to their behaviour. The behaviour can be bad, but the person is always good.

Neither is the aim of the behaviour equal to the action. The aim of the behaviour is always positive.

A person in a certain situation always chooses the best among the possibilities given by the idea. Although, there is not always enough information available to choose the best. Everything is in a person, of what is needed. The only task is that resources should be accessible when needed.

Everyone is capable to do everything. If someone is able to do something, we can make a model of his abilities, and teach it to others.

All behaviours are useful for something under some circumstances.

We always communicate. With all our senses we continuously receive and deliver signals, which are observed by other people. If there are no signals coming, it still has the same communicational value.

The meaning of the communication can be assessed by the quality of response. The point is not in what we say, but the reactions it calls forth from the other person.

The more opportunities of choice we have, the better it is.

There is no failure, only feedbacks that we can reach the same aim with other methods.

We can do anything, if we divide it into properly small steps.

Variability: in a system always the most flexible, most diverse behavioural element is the leader.

It was interesting to watch the face of the others as we were sitting in a semicircle, trying to read the reactions on each others face. How do our eyes, our face muscles, and eyebrows move? How do we crinkle our forehead? How much do our gestures and posture change?

We started to play a game. We sat in pairs, face to face with each other. We had to hide a coin in one of our fists. Our partner could watch this. First we had to show in which hand we put the coin then close our palm. My partner held his fists on his knees. I had to memorize his features and his posture, while with one of my hands I continuously had to point at his fist, in which he hid the coin. I had to ask the following several times:

– Is it here? – Then the answer came: – Yes, it is.

After a while, when I thought I managed to memorize and "take a photo" of his face, my partner put his hands behind him, and after a few seconds he showed me his fists again. I had to figure out – merely by paying attention to his face – that in which hand he had hidden the coin. During this I had to continuously ask: – Is it here? – And during that I had to point with my index finger to his fists. I had to watch his features, and compare it with the previous "photo".

Discussing the experiences, it turned out that one of our mates did not focus on the differences between the two faces, but concentrated on being sensitive to that metal, of which the coin was made. In this case to copper. They used a 10 cent euro coin. Summarizing her different experience, we assumed that for her the face examination didn't work out even once, so she solved the task in another way. She concentrated on the top of her right index finger to detect the copper. Since she was able to do this, she figured out ten times out of ten, in which fist is the coin.

After this we listened to several opinions about this. At the end our teacher said the following:

– Well, all right, she reached the aim in another way, but in the future try it like this – he stretched out his arm, and pointed his index finger upwards in an angle of forty–five degrees to the right, while he emphasized the expression "in the future". Only later on did we understand the essence of this.

– It is always important to follow the tasks according to the practice, since they are built up on each other. But I would like to mention some things related to this. Pay attention to me, and write it down.

SHE IS coming later on. Are you SURE ABOUT staying? She has a lot to do with HERSELF.

The fly didn't TAKE IT EASY being trapped in a spider's web. It fought for its life while the spider BEcame RELAXED MORE AND MORE. Live as you like, you HAVE to tide over hard times. You can still meet A NICE person, and you will surely see what a good EXPERIENCE it is. Finally make the bed not to MOVE anyMORE. I won't say it again. I don't want to say ALWAYS the same. You could work MORE at home! EVERYone likes one THING for sure, ice–cream. The summer IS GOING TO PASS again, but you can always buy it in every confectionary. You should come with me ONCE. ALWAYS have a handkerchief, my BEloved, KIND fellow. I LOVE that the junkman took away all the stuff. I confess this fact doesn't disturb ME.

I like it VERY MUCH. The lion told the ANIMALS the following: sometimes you NEED to have neutral relationships as well. Not everyone has TO BE LOVED.

We underlined all the words that were marked, and read them together. Reading these hidden instructions in the text, which we have been using since childhood, I realised that they had the strongest effect in our mother language. It is about creative or destructive impacts of words we say, which, for example, are known by number of politicians. A lot of people also emphasise certain words when they talk. They gesticulate to this in the same way, with this securing a condition that somebody wants to achieve in us, rousing fear or calming us down.

Certain schemes can be recognized in their speeches. For instance, the first time they tell us what to be afraid of – something that is imaginable. The result is generated fear, which can turn into a phobia.

It may be underpinned by false news published by the media. Then comes the damage caused in our home country, and in other countries we are in coalition with, and later on they mention the family and the children. After this we get to know who is for and against us. Several possibilities rise, which are underpinned by reports from intelligence service, well–known scientists, professors and other experts. After we are completely convinced of the fears they forced on us, and we can find alternative solutions for the problems, they call upon us to join forces to avoid further damages. All of these have to be voted of course. Of course, also the amount of money that is needed for this.

There may be civilian victims also, but it is going to be negligible compared to the terrible disaster that threatens our and other coalition countries – they say. We ask for all Churches to give us their blessings, as it happened in the Middle Ages, when Muslims blessed the holy war against Christians and vice versa.

We assert that only one God exists – OURS, WHO WAS BORN HERE. Nevertheless, all wars may be merely about a politician, who has the dictatorial ability for mass suggestion, and wants to conquer areas in a country, which "has the most dangerous threat to us", because there are industrial raw material as well.

Unfortunately, I have never heard such a reason for war between the most developed countries that either of them wants to build a pharmaceutical factory in Africa exclusively specialised for the AIDS disease, due to huge expected profit. Yet, internationally the number of patients might be the biggest on this continent.

In our everyday life we meet conditions which are set by different suggestions, and there are some we are waiting to happen, such as the disapproval of our boss when we are late for work in the morning.

Imagine the following: we arrive to our workplace half an hour later. Our boss comes to us with a nice smile. He greets us, and asks how we are. He shows interest in why we were late. And we tell him the truth without lying and making excuses. Then he replies:

– You know, you are one of the most valuable employees at our company so we don't worry if you are late or not. Shall we decrease your salary because of this? No. With all of your colleagues we would like, if you could work even better, more properly, and more precisely. How can we help you in this? I, as your boss, would like to do everything I can. Perhaps this kind of approach is new for you, but we would like to help. What can I do for you?

Maybe it seems to be utopian. For whom it is, I wish you a boss like this.

Unfortunately, every day we get positive and negative suggestions through the internet, television or radio. Picture, sound, emotion. These three are necessary to pick up on something. Television commercials in some cases are louder, compared to the movie we watched before. Billboards usually draw attention due to their size alone. In several cases sex is also used, implicitly targeted to buy the given product. Advertisers look for one sentence, one sound, one image, one emotion focusing on a certain social group, which can be the future customer of that particular product. It would be difficult to sell shampoo to bald people, but a hair–restorer product or a free first consultation of a hair transplantation clinic might be interesting.

Or let's think vice versa. Let's buy something out of season.

In wintertime we can buy swimming suits with 80% discount, or in summertime winter coats are available for half price.

What do you think about this? Do you stay with your washing powder, and toothpaste they recommend, or do you change to another one that is actually chosen by you. What do you pay attention to? The package or something else?

Once, our niece came to visit us. We were having our breakfast. I asked her what she wanted to eat. She said that she did not like turkey meat, and the cheap cold cuts on the table. I gave her the most delicious cold cuts made from turkey, which I found in the fridge. She took it. Ate it. I could see that she liked it. I asked her how it was.

– Very tasty – she replied.

– What a relief that you liked the expensive cold cuts made from turkey.

I saw her stunned face for several minutes after this. Till these days, when we meet, I always remind her of the PLACEBO chicken which was actually turkey.

How much do I pay for buying PLACEBO effects in shops? Where do I go shopping? I'm glad that with certain products sometimes I also have to buy the package, of which I surely gathered a great–sized wonderful waste mountain during my life.

One of my friends worked on a fishing boat in Italy for years. Until his first day he was a fanatic environmentalist. At that day three barrels full with old oil were thrown into the sea next to Sardinia. As his colleagues saw his anger, they tried to calm him down by saying this: "We always do it like this!"

If we'd put all the garbage that you threw out during your life into your house, would you be able to open the entrance door?

What do you think about the fact that communities emphasising the importance of a clean environment, build residential parks on the top of buried waste mountains, and later on they are surprised when the houses start to decay and several asthmatic, cancerous diseases occur among them and their children? Only the profit matters! I'm sure that people and their needs, which are essential for living, should be at the first place, followed by luxury items. PROFIT and MONEY come only at the end of the row.

I help my fellow–beings. The benefit is smaller, but free publicity is bigger contact, so I have more and more clients who need something from me. I don't pay for commercials. I help also clients who became friends of mine in the meantime – more money for me. More recognition, more energy. But unfortunately, it will only work well, if we solve real problems, and not call people's attention to fake necessities.

PICTURE, SOUND, EMOTION? Let's see what we can do with these. Let's sit in front of our TV, and turn off the sound. Watch only the screen. Is it colourful or black and white? When I sit in front of it where it is? At eye–level? Is it on my right or on my left? Up or down? I turned off the sound so I can't hear how loud the commercials are. But as I was watching the screen, I realised that there is 4/3 and 16/9 picture ratios as well. Very good. I reduce the size of the image and try to sit further. I can barely see it; I sent it away from me. It is a very small image. I imagine it in black and white. It is very small. Now I close my eyes, and slowly, very slowly I send it away from me. It became a very small, tiny dot. I can do the same with images of some negative experiences as well. If I can't remove them from myself, I step next to them and hit them with a giant hammer so that they break into millions of splinters, which by then are neutral to me.

I can do it as much as I want. This was my picture. Now it is absolutely indifferent. But if I want to clean up everything, all the remains, I can order my inner, imaginary cleaning crew as well, which has a tiny function. The small particles have to be cleared by small creatures since they are responsible for the cleaning of my vessels, all of my organs, my lungs, my kidneys and my intestines. They are small as the thousandth split part of a micromillimeter. They are never late from my body, and they work in a normal work time. There have paid vacations, holidays, premiums for Christmas and Easter, and any other reward that can be given. I guess I have to thank them for keeping me clean inside.

Learning from bad experiences, crushing their images, stays the image of a healthy, clean unit inside and outside of my body as well. Therefore I'm grateful every day for my small team, and as all good bosses do, the best of the bosses, who treat the assistants equally for a better cooperation I ask them:

– What do you guys need? New vitamins? Is there anyone who needs bio fruits, vegetables or meat? They always reply to a good and honest boss, me.

They tell me: now the coffee was too much, or the liquid was not enough today. Drink more before you go to bed. You need more vegetables and hot soup. Now a little rest and a good tea.

After that I can continue my activities with renewed energy. Because, you know, what you have found in yourself can be also found outside of you as a new environment. You only have to look for it. Open the screen of your radar, which has been closed till now. Listen, emerge from yourself, and look around, where is the harmony. If you need to do it, do what you need. Adapt to reach your goal. What is the aim? If it comes true, and you will see yourself there, in the moment of success, how will you feel? What is the picture that you see of yourself? Can you look out from yourself? Are you looking out of your body, or do you see yourself from the outside? Is the picture colourful or black and white? Do you hear voices? From where do you hear them? What exactly do you hear? Is it your own voice or does it belong to someone else? Is it a cacophony? Is it broken or clean? Is it DEEP or high?

My teacher asked me what kind of aim I can tell him that I want to reach.

– I want to fly – I replied.

– Are you sure?

– Yes, I am!

– Well, and what kind of higher aim would you achieve with this?

– I don't know – I said, embarrassed.

– Don't you think that your fellow–beings would realise that you are just flying in the sky topsy–turvy?

– Probably, they would. But I can still have dreams like this. I want to fly without all sorts of devices, such as the Indian yogis, who according to my readings, rose up from the ground and flew when they wanted.

– Well, all right. Then let's do a practice with such an aim with one of your colleagues. Any volunteers?

The lawyer raised her hand.

– Julia, do you wish to do this?

– Yes, I do.

Julia was approximately a forty–fifty year–old lady, but she didn't look more than twenty–six. She was a well–situated, intelligent, smart woman. Later on we became good friends. She was the first lady who asked me on a date. We walked arm in arm. On that day we talked about many things, then suddenly she changed the topic:

– Stephen, I'm sorry that I'm not twenty years younger – she said, as she came to a halt. In the next moment she gave a kiss on the middle of my forehead.

I stopped for a moment, and wondered. I looked into her two beautiful green eyes, and sighed deeply.

– I'm sorry as well, but for not being twenty years older.

We both laughed hardly on this.


– One of you has to be the observer, then you switch the roles. There will be a questioner, somebody who makes up an aim, and an observer – said the instructor, then continued:

– If it is possible, the aim shouldn't be too difficult and evident for the first time. It should be smaller and easier instead. Put up the right questions. It is very important to pay attention, evaluate and compare external gestures to features on the face, to assess if the person will reach the desired aim. All right, let's start.

# Sixth Chapter

There's a typical family strategy from moms and dads live when they notice that their child is lying.

Smaller things only go with changes in the facial expressions. However, bigger lies can trigger twitching, shaking movements of limbs while being questioned. The result can be turned out from the difference between the normal behaviour and from the one when they are questioned.

Similar methods can be used during interrogations at police stations, where first as a psychological effect, nightmares of the possibly worst punishment are exaggerated for the person who is being interrogated. Later on – after several psychological signs of his fear can be seen– the worst future punishment starts to soften, together with the severity of the penalty, until the person starts to cooperate maximally. Here, however, we have to say a few words about the dragon which exists in every human. It can be called like this, or evil.

How can you picture it? What are its colour, shape, and size? Can you communicate with it? What is it saying to you? Is it a friend or an enemy? Where is it in your body? If it is in you, what do you think, do you need it? Do you usually talk with it or not? If it is outside of you, why did you disown it?

The dragon of my ten–year–old son sleeps above his stomach. He just finished eating and brushing his teeth. Yet, it is also a dragon child in size, as my son. His rabbit is on his left wrist; his tiger is under his stomach. We need to know that during reincarnations we go through the entire so–called Darwinian phylogeny as in forms of

45

plants and animals. Thus, all existing organisms can be found in our bodies. If I focus, I can find all the animals. The development of all lives and life forms are equally important to me.

The head of my favourite cobra is resting on top of my head. Its tail runs along my spine, going down to the end of it. Its two eyes are above mine. It's always motionless. It always gives me huge power; we see everything clearly, and tell the experiences to each other. When my dear dragon enlarges to its full size, it looks very similar to Godzilla for me. It only becomes enormous when someone, or something is preparing to do an evil thing against life in my surroundings, although, it knows that the point, and the essence of this life is not LOVE, ACCEPTANCE, TOLERANCE, which overlap religions, minorities, and everything, but money became our god now, which determines our everyday life globally. It is often very sad, because of this. These times it tells me. I listen to it, and I'm happy that it can be with me. These times it curls up into a small ball, and without any sound, as a small youngling that just came out from the egg, it lays under my heart to its place in peace.

# Seventh Chapter

Should we set an aim? Why for? Why? For whom is this going to be good? For my smaller, or larger environment? If I get there in the future, where I'd like to, won't I change negatively to myself, according to my present view of life? What will other people say about me? Will I be successful? What is success for me? Can the amount of money be significant for me? Will one more zero at the end of my bank account make me satisfied? Can the amount of bought items make me happy? Does the fact make me happy that I know if somebody asks me to buy them something, I am capable of buying it? Can the admiration of earthly objects, things generate devotion towards them? Do I devote to my ability that what I, my family and my fellow human beings really need, I could get in the right time for their and my development? What's more important to me, the finished product or the ability?

A typical case of the prodigal son: maybe I can get everything, but for me the ability is important. The same when I was taught to tie my shoelaces. It is safety that I tie another bow on the top of it, so that it won't loosen while I'm wearing it. I loosen it, when I want to!

Unfortunately, not all our activities are carried out so safely, so easily. A lot of people are very nervous before school exams; they panic, get anxious, eat less, learn more, and sometimes stay awake very late at night.

It's rare that they don't get to know in time, when they are going to have the exam. They don't pay attention to tie their shoelaces daily, to study regularly, every day. Although, I have to know: my Lord teaches something to me every day. It is only that everyone stores it a different way in his or her mind. How late or early does the old information, which you need right now to satisfy an inner or outer pressure, get to your consciousness? Are you nervous or are you sitting in entire peace, surprising even your examiners?

I know that I won't be able to tell the thesis I got perfectly, but I'm sitting at this desk, where people in front of me are putting up questions, like I'm at home in my dining room after a weekend lunch. I'm already full. My stomach is having a rest, I'm relaxed, I've just drunk a glass of mineral water, and while looking in my teacher's eyes I'm waiting for the questions.

I've set a high goal for myself, and I transferred the feeling of a "safe environment", a so–called RESOURCE to a place, where others are nervous. I passed the exam. How many everyday resources do I have, which I can transfer to even more risky situations? Is it me that generates panic or someone else? Can it be an aim for someone that I must sweat, be nervous with a knot in my stomach on the most important exam of my life?

After years pass, I can see the whole thing in another way. I can think of the fact that millions of other people are also doing similar tests during their life, even in elderly age. They also pass. Over the years the panic disappears from my fading, blurring, shrinking pictures. Later on I just wave my hand. Come on, this was also done. Shoes are tied again. I can tie them beforehand as well!

# Eighth Chapter

Can devoted, pure love, which accepts everyone and everything, be my aim?

First send these kinds of your thoughts in yourself, to yourself, to the parts in you. There will be plenty of them, you'll see.

Look for the behaviours in your body, which can carry you through your goals! There will be good, and bad ones as well. Accept them, and talk to all of them equally, if you can! Somehow like this: as you are in me, you are equally important to me. I'm glad for this long awaited meeting. From now on we will talk more, and revalue a lot more things, which happened to us in the past. The aim of some positive behaviour can be reached with mutual understanding, with a behaviour that keeps my system in a healthy unit. Probably these things won't be a big change for me.

I was a drug addict and an alcoholic. Before that I smoked for years in imagination, every day several times. Even now I can't stop the ambition of provoking these feelings evoked by narcotics. I love to fly relaxed, relieved, with an almost unconscious body. I love everything and everyone, wherever I am. I send my unconditional love, and my good intentions to everywhere, to all worlds, to all living things of all worlds. In fact, by the time I get there, along the long journey my friend will introduce me to his friends, who become my new friends. They introduce me, like when new acquaintances want to get to know somebody. Like a pleasant evening or afternoon tea in the old England centuries ago.

It is an interesting feeling to arrive to a foreign atmosphere with a good will, and to meet even more positive minds and souls with the help of the universal bonds, and network of love.

Am I looking for someone? I can find that person the same way as on the internet. I type in my favourite searcher, LOVE, which finds me the address, which I open through the help of the presented connection.

I move at full speed on the World Wide Web, without the knowledge of time and space. Enormous amount of information opens in front of me. Magnificent sight, sounds and huge lexical knowledge. I can find anything easily. It's a money–based system. Advertisements appear on huge surfaces, we can surf between different pages with shared attention. They can tempt us to buy things. And we do buy some of them. It connects the entire world, on which we live. But you know this is small for me! The World Wide Web is small, because it is "only" for the Earth. But what is beyond that?


At the beginning of my night "journeys", a sixteen–year–old girl told me that at nights she consciously stepped out herself, and moves only in her room, because there she felt safe.

The first time she got up out of her bed, she was surprised of her silver cord. Sometimes the girl went for a small walk in her room at night. In the meantime, she had a look at the timetable for the next day, and put some books into her bag. When she finished, she even looked at her watch to see how much time is left till she has to wake up. First she doubted these actions carried out on astral planes. She believed them to be dreams. But then she figured out something that she repeated several times, because she was not able to understand with a normal, rational mind what was happening to her. She picked up a book in the evening, which she didn't need next day in school. Before going to bed she put this book in her bag, then on astral plane took it out, and in her dreams she put it on her desk, which she cleared before bedtime. The selected book was lying on the desk alone every morning, when she experimented with this. Thus she had to believe her acquired ability. She didn't know where she learned this, and why she is able to do this. Who allows her to do this anyway?

The first time I saw her in her room on astral plane, viewing from above, her body colours were flickering. She was frightened of me: it was her first time to see a person move around like her. That night we talked a lot. I told her that she didn't do anything new. What's more, she is following the right direction to save money, and not to pay to many travel agencies.

– Where do you want to go? – I asked. – Really badly? Tell me a place!

– I want to see the Statue of Liberty in New York – she said.

– I think it is boring. It stands in one place among boring skyscrapers. The rushing people of New York are running around with anti–life thoughts in their mind, and interesting astral colours of their quite abnormal money–grubbing, as they were animals that gone crazy. Come on; let's walk instead on the Hawaiian beach, in the sand, under the palm trees. It is daytime there now, but believe me, no one will see us, only the ones with the same abilities we have. But they are good friends. Stand here beside me, hold my hand, and think that you are becoming a small sphere of light.

– What is that like? – She asked.

– I'll show you. Take me in your hands!

I shrank, and then we kept on talking telepathically.

– Now it's your turn – I said. – If you are afraid, close your eyes, we're almost there.

She followed me. She became even a smaller light sphere than me. We could go faster. I really had to open my eyes. We were there too fast. If we convert, our journey lasted around fifteen seconds. We stopped at the shore. I felt fright and fear beaming through her hands. This was her first long journey. Since then she has done other ones elsewhere. I unpacked my astral body to a normal human size, while doing so I was continuously holding her hand.

– You can crawl out, I'm already outside – I said.

– Yes. What is it like?

– How do you like it?

– It is pretty, very pretty!

– That's what I was talking about. Let's take a walk! As you see, no one can sense us here now.

It was strange for her that the tourists moving on the beach in the normal dimension didn't even notice us.

– You'll get used to it! Don't forget this: before you go anywhere, two steps forward, and one backward. Stop, look around and think! Take potential dangers into account! Now I take care of your silver cord, if it tears, you die! In your mind protect it from any conceivable external impacts, which you can imagine. Meditate a lot on this! This is the most important. Your ability was born with you, mine is learned. I learned every day what you got as a gift, so use it smartly. I know that you are a talented student; you are the top of the class. I looked into your school–report before you prepared yourself for the travelling. Talk about your skills only to people who deserve it. External signs will let you know who is suitable for this. Maybe your third eye will open as well. If so, learn the meaning of the differences between colours, and interpret them. For example, you will be able to recognize diseases, truthfulness etc.

We talked a lot while walking on the beach. We didn't leave any footprints in the sand, but only in our hearts.

– We have to go – I said. – Due to the time difference. I quickly write down my phone number, and leave it on your desk. Please call me tomorrow after school, when you arrive home.

– All right – she said.

We curled into two small white light spheres again, and went home. After we arrived, we put on our normal figure. I wrote my phone number on a piece of paper. We said goodbye. The next afternoon I came home late. There were three messages on my answering machine.

– I am the girl from the Hawaiian Islands yesterday. Call me back! My number is...

Second message: – Is this really your number or are you just fooling with me? Call me back! My phone number is...

Third message: – I've been thinking a lot. I do not know what to believe. I may have only dreamt it all. Call me!

I picked up the receiver and dialled. Her mother answered. She called her daughter to the phone. I heard her asking her daughter:

– Who is this? Your new boyfriend?

– No. Not at all.

– Then how does he know our home phone number? I told you not to give it to your boyfriends!

– He's not my boyfriend!

– Then who is it?

– I'll tell you, Mom. Give me the phone!

– Well, here you are! But then you have to tell me everything. I don't want you to do something stupid by mistake.

– Oh, Mommy, don't stress! Everything is all right!

– Hi! I am your fellow–traveler.

– Hi! And I'm your travelling companion.

– How are you?

– I'm fine, and you?

– Me too.

– Forget my number and I forget yours. I think you don't need to have a phone, if you want to talk to me. Look for me! If you remember my colours, you'll find me! What do you think? Are you wondering about the things that happened at night?

– Was there anything strange for you?

– Yes. You didn't bring me to the Statue of Liberty.

– You can go as well. I have been there many times, it is boring for me. What else would you like? I guess you should have a rest for a couple of days now. Meet you some time later. Upload your batteries. Go to the forest or to a stream. Walk a lot. Gain energy, think! Compose positive goals! Then we meet. All right?

– Okay – she said.

– Be nice and very happy – I said and hung up the phone.

Since then I have never met a sixteen–year–old girl with such a mature and clear mind.

# Ninth Chapter

I go to school every day whether I'd like to or not. I go to the school of life. I leave in the morning after waking up, and I always learn something whether I want to or not. Then later I remember back – or don't. Many times I don't understand why that day was needed.

This was also a regular day like any other one. No variety. Always the same. Never ending replay on TV as well. I'm tired of my neighbours too. They always do the same thing. They always park in front of the driveway. In the mornings I always have to honk the horn so that they come out, and park a few meters farther away. And they're the ones who are pissed after, if I wake them up. Am I even needed here? Or would it be better, if I died? Why do I have to do the same thing for decades? I will live worse from year to year anyway. There will be nothing new, just the usual everyday stuff. The world doesn't need me. I'll die instead! I am full of problems, which I can't solve. Nobody helps me. I can't tell my problems to anyone, no one listens to me. No one can help, there is only one way:  I MUST DIE! IT SOLVES EVERYTHING! There's going to be enough money out of my life insurance even after my funereal. My children will be able to spend it on meaningful things. Maybe it will be better for them as well. I'm always listening to them criticising me. Why do I earn so little money? Why don't I spend more time with them? In this way, I won't have to listen to this anymore.

How should I end myself? What is the surest method? Poison, knife, or shall I jump down from somewhere? Shall I step in front of a moving truck? Which one is the best?

NOT THIS ONE! NONE OF THESE ARE GOOD ENOUGH.

# Tenth Chapter

## Astral world

After, in the normal earthy existence, I graduated from an evening school, and finished a one–year obligatory military service, I still dreamt a lot about the army. Here, I learned that the most widely used machine gun is the Kalashnikov. The ratio of this Russian miracle is more than sixty percent next to similar weapons in the world. Quite a lot. I came to like this weapon because of its simplicity. Actually, its soul is a very long spring, which enables it to fire off precisely up to a kilometer.

Many times, when we cross the threshold between conscious and unconscious, there is also a control built into the door. Only those things come into the conscious world from the astral one, which don't hinder our conscious, everyday activities. Many people try to explain the things they experienced during their sleep with the help of the so–called dream–books. The events can be also negative and positive, as well as their explanations. But the most important things are the control and the openness towards my internal parts, which enable me to pick up a certain behaviour. They are parts of me, they work for me. The ultimate goal is sure behind their actions, it is to give me a good feeling. If I want to go on a date, and I'm standing in front of the wardrobe, looking for what to wear, everything is just because I want to please my partner. It may happen in the meantime that I like none of my clothes, but the aim is that I would like to please my new partner even more. I would like to show her something more, greater, better about and from myself. My clothes also belong to do this. I dress up with a positive satisfaction. In the end, it turns out that the date was successful. Then weekdays come, and I get back in my everyday clothes. Days pass by, one after another. I find the T–shirt that I wore on the first date, and I wonder.

When will I have a first date feeling again? How many years do I need for this?

# Eleventh Chapter

Most mornings I wake up with the feeling that I have to go to school. It happened one Wednesday. It was half past six. I looked across the room searching for my schoolbag and study books. I stepped to my desk, and pulled out the drawers. I didn't find books in neither of them. I sat down on my chair desperately. I glanced at my desk searching with my eyes for the timetable, although I didn't find that either. It came into my mind that I only had 10 minutes left till leaving, till that I have to collect all my things or I'll be late!

I think my first class will be mathematics, yesterday it was literature. Few of my classmates were absent. The teacher sent me for them at night. When? At night? What kind of school is this? What is lying in my hands? The newspaper from yesterday. I was searching for the first page. I have to find the date! Oh my God! Is this the newspaper from yesterday? What kind of date is this? I've gone crazy! I have to go to school! If I am absent or late, the punishment will be big. I want to study! I am a top student out of every subject; I only get the best grades. I memorise everything at the first hearing and can repeat it back, I can even imitate the teacher's intonation, if I have to. My homeroom teacher said that my brain is like a picture and voice recorder built in with unlimited memory. And what am I doing now? Sitting in my chair and brooding over yesterdays date. It's impossible! Where am I? In what time? What's happening to me? Maybe yes! I don't understand the date! I have to find a calendar! According to this I finished my last school five years ago, although I remember that I have examinations in plenty of subjects. Some lessons will be left out! The colour analysing of the astral body, because in this life it is not needed. What? What happened? I don't understand the whole thing! I go to school, but where? What kind of subject is "Improvement of imagination ability individually for the protection of our own silver cord for the accomplishment of safe astral travelling"? I have to learn this also! What can I cut a cord with? The scissor is which I think about first. Knife, sword, sabre, dagger, scythe, spade, and every object with a cutting edge. It can be even burnt with everything that causes fire, flames. A fire spitting dragon can burn it, and maybe can get hold of my soul. Then I'll die and leave this earthly world.

I'll die, if I want to! How many times do I have to open a door? Or should I ask the guardian of the door to open it for me? Or is it enough, if he sees that I'm coming, then he'll open it determined and without a request, as I'd be at the entrance of one of those big hotels? My subconscious also has a guard. A very important individual. In I go every time with a clean mind, out I come yet with the memories of my covered distance which come clearly or in a coded way, which I thought was a dream at first, but later I recognized that these are established facts! The consciousness guardian of my mind standing at the door is trying to fulfil its task with the knowledge of both of my consciences, exchanging the information, while paying attention to my reactions.

This school was too much for me. It was a military school. After the completion of it I felt like I'm on one of the sites of the World War II. In a trench, next to me my partners. In their hands also a Kalashnikov. Thick bullet shower, above the ditch flying grenades explosive voice as they hit the ground and the blunt noise of a few limbs thudding to the buried out sand from the detonation. The sight of ripped off legs and arms! Blood flowing from arms which have been torn of by fragments of the bombshell! Why for?

I woke up again. I was dreaming again. One day went past in my normal life then again these dreams come. I'm afraid to go to sleep. Very afraid! Why do I have to do this? Why can't I be up at night also? Maybe then I wouldn't dream such stupid things!

Slowly I'll go mad, I'm not sane, I'll get into an insane asylum sooner or later.

– Calm down. I am your doorman, not your gate keeper – said a voice from inside.

– Maybe the curriculum is a bit much, but now you are learning the basic things: the combat, the cooperation in team. Remember? Two weeks ago we rewarded and forwarded it to be a sergeant. Neither then did you know what was happening to you. You thought then as well that you've gone crazy. There's no problem, believe me! You study outstandingly in the astral school. You know, even the application form is hard to gain here. You know the first step of this is to clean your own energy centre, your chakras which come hand in hand with changing your attitude with things. With this your behaviour will be altered, but the environment in which you live will stay the same. After a while somebody will recognize the amount of changes which happened within you. Your faith in things will also change; with God you will have a different relation. Maybe you will know the way to him, but be careful; you will get powers which are a great deal of number and powerful. You will have many new abilities. These are existing coded powers in all human beings, which do not work when operated by own intentions. They take you to your own existence.

If you use it in the matter of a loving community, you will get even more energies back. You can receive energies in an everlasting amount. Maybe you will never become ill. Sorry, I said it in the wrong way on purpose, now I'll tell it in a positive way: you will always be in a healthy unit with yourself and with the worlds around you, in which, if you send positive, loving, accepting thoughts, you will receive it back. Far away, anywhere, your thoughts and your energy are always ahead of you and take the news that once you will get there. They will wait for you. If you arrive, you will have many friends, and the friends of your friends will also be your friends by time. Remember the Yin and the Yang, black and white. You do something good; somebody does the same bad thing against you somewhere, but the world still heads uniformly on the road of improvement. Because fundamentally, improvement is the essence anywhere, in any life horizon of living or inanimate beings. You can be as the sun, which's radiating warmth penetrates everything again and again. It rises and settles down. We think that it's just for us. The sun always shines the same way, pouring its warmth, but we still need the night–time, as the day–time. This is how everything is complete. Let in the energy of love through the snake on top of your head and radiate it in thought through your body to your fellow–beings with the usage of every nerve ending during the daytime. In the stage of development they are the closest to you. Then carry the energy to everything else, every living being. Many elderly people love their own dog more than the family–members whom don't care about him or her. However, if they turned their loving thoughts towards them also, many things could change. Be one of the suns, and radiate from yourself love towards everybody, even towards the intoxicated drug user lying around, whom doesn't know about his or herself. He or she is also the part of the world, because he or she is there. If it was not needed, he or she wouldn't be there. He or she is on that human stage of development precisely where he or she needs to be and everything else and everybody else also. You cannot accomplish the school of life, if you leave out classes! Everybody is exactly where they have to be for their life experiences, of which after gaining you can step forward.

Few people can't even find their subconscious, not that the entrance of it! With the doorman, with me, not much people talk. At these kind of schools only a few people are registered. I'll tell a few subjects. But before... You surely know that who accomplishes university can work out high school tasks much more easily? This means that if you accomplish the subjects intended for you on astral plane, then in normal life your being will be simpler and easier. Find the parallels and identity, then you can start thinking simple. What is here, is there also! If something goes well here, then it will work there also! So the subjects are: object–movement, the modification of your own shape and size, imagination development, movement of objects from one distance to the other, mindreading, astral colour analysis for sicknesses and lies, flying, astral travelling, moving through objects, etc.

What gets into your mind? There is more! Not all is needed for you!

Well, are you using it for your own purpose? For material profit, or will you be a sun radiating love instead? Which one do you choose? Later you will have time to answer; we will speak other times again. By then I hope you accept every part of you, and you can communicate with them constructively. Don't forget either of your parts; every one of them is equally important as your hand or your foot. You can say thanks everyday for every drop of your blood, because it is in you. Absolutely! Weird? Is not! Think. Are you okay? Everything fine? Go to work, at night the school awaits you. Now you became a sergeant, you are rewarded. You got it at a great feast. I'm interested how much time you need for your lieutenant colonel rank. Till then you will fight many times. Improve your abilities, but the most important is to keep your mind clean. It's fine to have a thought about everything, but you should be the owner of these. When you say, this should end now, then it should end! No more! Think about something else! About what you want to! A thought can come and go as the wind. Or it can catch you up as a tornado for a while then throw you down to the ground. Then you can hit yourself very badly. It will hurt.

Maybe the so–called love is the same, although I'm not sure, I have never been in love. You are up above the clouds somewhere. You see everything through pink eyeglasses; you go into a different world. You only look at the other person. You're with him or her. You breathe, sleep together, love each other, every limb of one another. You feel that in the other you find everything that is needed to fulfil your world. You can barely wait for him or her to call you up, see, hear his or her voice. You want to hug him or her as soon as possible, again and again. You think that only with that person can your life be fulfilled. You will make plans together for the future. Laughing, cheerful, and happy will you two look forward for the upcoming new things. In that person you found happiness for a life. You want to grow old, raise children, live your everyday life. Life through good, rejoice together for the wonderful things. Help him or her in everything which is a bad or sad experience. You will help each other to make these happenings positive. You have to be prepared for negative things also.

What kind of affect does it have on one another? How much will you be stressed or nervous? What will you do? Shout and throw plates to the floor in the kitchen or calmly sit down in the middle of the room, thinking through all the possibilities to minimize the upcoming losses? Or what do you do? How will your partner react? Always the same way?

You feel with the years passing by that you become more and more unaffected in these situations of conflict. Do you even know him or her? Or do you just think you know? What do you know about him or her? What do you think you know about him or her? How did that person act with you in a similar situation and how does this person act now? Do you feel the difference between the two reactions? If yes is the answer, than what exactly is it? Do you live in a good marriage with yourself? You know here, where I am the door–keeper you have much more selves. Here are all the beings from your previous life: all the animals, plants and humans whom have already been born. I'm interested, if you can find them; and by making contact and having a conversation with them, how much will they build your current individual? Where will you look for them? Don't go far! What is inside, is found outside also. You know, public transportation is found here also. At the same time, everybody chooses their own vehicle. Some people travel with subway, some by car, and there are those super managers who travel with private airplanes on the wings of their imagination. Others don't travel there either, but use video–telephones – this is telepathy.

I almost forgot, or not!? It is important for you to learn the upcoming subject also. It's a bit complex, but I will like what you will write about it in your doctoral dissertation. It will be too long. But I'll tell you the essence of it. Even if it is not needed for you to see and examine the aura for your conscious self, your unconscious self in your consciousness can still memorize and analyze the colour of your fellow–beings and save those in its memory as a picture. Remember: your memory can be continuously increased. Maybe scientist can detect only a few percent of brain usage, because in the other parts the pictures of your previous life's are stored, so it can be seen for those whom are worthy of it. What were you in your previous life?

Some day you will ask yourself. In the right time you will get an answer. Sorry about the detour. So I was saying that you can examine somebody's aura colour and remember it. Pay attention to their energy centre, how it turns. Which one is slower, which one is faster? You can get to know many things. For example, you can recognize sooner than usual a woman who would like to make love or is pregnant. Even when that individual doesn't know about it. Many people who have power to, consider where they would like to be born. Why exactly there? What will they have to do in their next life? They still remember the previous one, by those memories, or for selfish purposes, or for the interest of other people maybe they will choose parents. You will have a daughter and a son. You will already know your son for about 1000 years, your daughter for about 500 years. There is much information. Your son will be your best friend. He is the one, whom will wait for you for a long time, but you will still be with him. Your daughter will love you as nobody before. But you have to let go both of them whilst being by their side. Everything is solvable. Even this. At least you know the people around you. The aura tells you everything. Even the lies. Other people are in that spiritual stage where they have to be. They are just learning. There are those who look for something different on the internet. The dream of the cyber space. People without faces and names feed you with empty promises, because anything can be done on the internet. You can hide, put your flaws behind a disguise, damp them, lie about everything. Maybe the other person does the same.

Have you ever thought about it, how honest do you have to be to other people? And to yourself? Sadly the answer is overwhelmingly simple. In the same amount.

Be honest in every minute and tell the truth! Therefore the parts in you can't contradict with each other.

You tell yourself, you are hungry. You go to the

kitchen, but you don't eat. You just stand in one place. Thinking about lemons. You can feel its taste in your mouth. You know it's in the fridge, but you still don't open the door of it, you don't want to take it out. By the thought of lemon you get thirsty. You drink a cup of water. Put down the cup and go back to the room. You went out to eat, in the end you drank. You get an error message from your body, like a computer which is programmed to lie. Your computer starts to hate the programmer. You start to tear apart from the inside. From your birth your parts are bonded tightly. You have to make these even stronger!

Maybe you can wish for a floating good feeling. Just a bit. Stress reducing relaxation. You start with a sedative or some drugs. Slowly you sense the nice feeling. There's a lot of stress, you know it; this is good for you, because this will unwind you. Much money is needed for it.

You start taking away the money from your parents. They don't know what's up with you. You shut them out of your life. You start lying; the whirl of it pulls you into the deep. You don't remember what you said yesterday, when they asked you, where were you? You know, everything is within you. The universe inside you is so great that it can't even be expressed in light–years. All the ability, opportunity is within you. Just inside you and the other person. Find the method, so that all the people around you, whom you ever get connected to in any way, gets to see life more positive, has the life energies flow more freely.

Go all along the street! Who faces you while strolling? The old lady is toddling with a walking cane in front of you. How do you think about her?

– Break your leg on the first jutting out ice.

Or you look at her and think: God watch out for her health for at least the next 20 years. Give strength for her to play even with her great–grandchildren!

Pregnant women on the street.

Well they knocked this one up! Great! It's sad that it wasn't me! Stupid bitch, like all the other ones. Gobbled up the semen! It does no good!

Or: I see how her belly is getting round. I hope she'll give birth to a healthy, pretty baby. Her husband will always be by her side. It will be a joy for him also to hold the baby first in his hands; maybe even a teardrop will spring into his eyes. He will think: My child. I will give him everything I can, and you also, mother of my child. I love both of you very much.

– I give you this child from myself because this is how much I love you! –Says the mom, then they hug each other.

What do you wish for the people facing you on the street? I have an idea! On the street wish somebody something good, then start chatting with that person! I bet that person will communicate with you positively. I'm sure. Although, completely explicit external signs can be exceptions. But if you know and believe that love above religions and the one God, that all the existing religions mention, is one and the same, then maybe you can feel more inner power within yourself. You can even smile. Smiles heal. Heals depression for sure. And laugh is a remedy. The cheapest. You don't have to find an insurance agency for this. Let everyday be something you can smile on, than later on laugh at. Let everyday be a good day! You know, in the desert if we only have a half glass of water, we're happy for that too, because it's half full. In the kitchen, by the water tap, you only get a half empty glass. Just the environment and needs are different. The half glass of water is always the same!

In the morning when you step out the front door and the sun is in your eyes again, you can say: ouch, it's blinding me. Then again you can say: I love the sun rays!

The sun is still the same! You know why you were forwarded to be a sergeant?

(I heard this amount of information approximately under one second with telepathy)

– No, no I don't know – I replied.

The doorkeeper went on:

– Many times we sent you to destroy demons and incubuses, because you are capable of it. These beings that are stuck in different planes of life, because they are not ready yet to develop, were hunting you and trying to damage your silver cord. But you were able to keep it and strengthen all your abilities. The best was when one of the incubuses tried to fight you face to face. He shot arrows towards you. First you jumped away. You tried to talk to him. First he didn't reply. You tried to question him, why he was trying to kill you. You told him that this was unnecessary. On this he became furious, got even more irritated. He shot even more arrows towards you. You were getting bored with this. Then something came into your mind. You surrounded him as a big clear sphere. He was very surprised. He stopped the arrow shooting. He stood and looked at his self in the middle of the sphere. You told him:

– How do you want to fight against something that surrounds you? I stay in this form as long as I want. Your form cannot be changed. Don't fight with something that is around you, it's not worth it. I accept you as you are! Think!

You used simple words then also, like always, it was understandable for him. You said you didn't feel like a winner, neither as a looser. You have a conscious life in the earthly world. Even there it is not worth fighting the things that surround you. You have to accept them and live further on while adapting to these things. With these few sentences you dismantled him. It was a very strong incubus. The right hand of death. The slave of Devil and Hell on that plane, where the souls who wish to be born are kept back with intended purpose, not even giving them the opportunity. They collect their life energies in one place and try to vegetate on those onward. Development can only happen in the material world, where you live. In Hell it doesn't work. There the souls just rub along. After a long time will those come out again, who are accidently released. They have to go through a long, bitter road and life planes to receive the opportunity of rebirth. So this is why you got that rank.

# Twelfth Chapter

I woke up.

I went to work. Instead of the usual job, we had to carry doors and windows, which weighed about 70–80 kilos, to the floors of a four story high, newly built building. Sadly, there were no elevators, and the stair landings were so tight that only two persons could carry it. Around noon my back started to hurt. I suggested to my colleague that we should change. Now I went in front, and he came behind me, that was how we carried the door. He agreed, then he said, he was waiting for me to ask him, because who is in the bottom carries the bigger weight. Then he gave me a malicious smile. At night, by the time I got home, my whole back was in pain. After dinner and taking a shower, I went to bed immediately. Didn't need any sleeping pills. Around midnight I woke up because my whole body was shaking and my back–spine was in great pain. I could barely move. I had to call my neighbours and the doctor also, who said that I lifted far too much and overworked my muscles. I got some painkillers, he suggested that I should be took out to the bathroom, put under the shower and should be bathed with some lukewarm water till my muscles loosen up a bit, because I could only move my own limbs with big pain. According to him, I overstrained all my muscles, and now I don't have muscular strain, but I totally wearied myself down. It was a miracle that I could go home.

From midnight till four in the dawn, two people were keeping me standing, on my two sides, by propping me from my armpits, and my third neighbour was holding the shower rose continuously, letting the water flow on me. I tried to move my limbs whilst having the shower. By five in the morning I was able to walk on my own, without any help. I laid down to rest a little. I thanked my neighbours for the help.

After a few hours I got thirsty. I got up. Started going towards the kitchen, by the fifth step I collapsed in the hallway, but I was able to catch the doorknob. I collapsed as if I were totally drunk, although I was completely sober. Under the influence of the painkillers I was a bit stunned. I recalled yesterday. We repeatedly had arguments with our boss and colleagues, why couldn't we solve this hard work a different way. The boss defended himself by saying that this was a deadline job; we didn't have time to install an elevating equipment or to rent a crane. This was the fastest solution in this situation. So let's not argue, work instead, so we can finish earlier – he said. Of course, he didn't help.

I was sitting in the hallway, with one hand hanging on the knob of the door. I took out my cell phone from my pocket. Sent a text message to my boss, saying that I can't go to work for a while because, according to my doctor, I overweighed my muscles and now, after collapsing, I'm lying on the floor of my hallway and writing these few lines. In the morning, at the time of work starting, I got the following call:

– What is this, that today nobody can come to work, who was carrying yesterday? Are you guys having a conspiracy against me? What is this, strike? You don't need the job? When can we wait for you? – The questions were just pouring!

– I'll take you the medical papers when I will be able

to work. Now I'm lying on the floor of the hallway for an hour now because I can't stand up. I'm taking the medication the doctor prescribed; otherwise I'd have awful pain – I answered.

– It's good if we can count on you. Call me up one–two days before. As far as I can see, a few orders have to be postponed. Get better as soon as possible! – With this he hanged up.

I needed two weeks to gain back my strength. Day by day I grew stronger! The first week I was afraid to go out of the house alone. I was afraid I'd trip somewhere and wouldn't be able to stand up. Or if I asked help from a stranger, he would think I'm drunk or a druggie and would walk past without any pity. At the beginning it was hard in a closed house alone. I imagined what it would be like to live in a wheelchair, live as a handicapped in a house that isn't transformed in such a manner, that from the wheelchair all articles of personal use would be within reach. One of the questions from my friend, whom was an insurance agent, came into my mind. He was able to establish many accident insurances with one sentence:

– If you, Sir, accidently – sadly not even God knows – got into a wheelchair for a while, and had to live like that, what do you think, how many centimetres lower would we have to put your upper kitchen–cabinet for you to reach it safely? How much would that job cost you?

He was a very successful agent. He projected ahead the picture of a life with limited abilities, then he clearly asked a question of the change of that lifestyle. Surely the solution was simple! Get a life insurance. This is what it's figured out for! With money everything can be solved! I was shut into a house. As I would be handicapped. Imagined myself into a wheelchair.

How do I move around in the hallway? Everything is really too high for me in the kitchen. I can't wash the dishes. I can't get into the wardrobe–room! How would I cook? Oh my God, I wouldn't be able to get down the stairs to the corner store, but not even to get up to the house. The details of an interesting new lifestyle came into my mind, with all the tiny elements of it. For days I was brooding about what is it like to live in a wheelchair. What kind of a life can a person have who isn't able to stand up? With what admiration can he look at his fellow–beings? What a miracle it is that nothing worse happened to me? In the doctors opinion it could have happened. One week later he visited me. He verified that I was getting better, but I still needed a week for my physical recovery. Then everything would be alright. One other thing: I have to get stronger mentally also. Consciously wanting to get stronger. Maybe this is the most important – he said.

Well, yes, I thought, while I'm lying, my unconscious self soars. He doesn't need a body, just to stay alive. My body is the harbour in the sea of aether. For anchor I use my silver cord, which I protect with my imagination. More than one protection membrane surrounds it. It resists every exterior attack! Military weapons, chemicals, heat, sound, materials, and against every other similar natured attack it resists perfectly. Without the imagination of this I don't even set off. After I untie my boat from the side of the landing stage, I always look at the quality of my cord. Invisible infrared laser–system detects even the possibility of damage. Don't even have to mention my friends, with whom we keep an eye on each other in this unearthly clan, family. We notice even the slightest change. The starting point is the body! If you know who lives where, than at night, after going to sleep you can fly off to him. You can check, whether he is at home? Does he want to talk to you? Or you could just leave him a message, or send an email also, of course with telepathy.

I don't understand why people are so attached to these electronic devices used nowadays in keeping contact with each other, when we would just need to train our own mind. First step is, when you know that somebody is going to call you, because previously you were just thinking about that person. You involuntarily tuned up in your mind to the brain waves of that person. You really wanted him or her to call you up, and the person did. You send an email. You know that he or she won't respond. And that person doesn't. Doesn't the usage of these electronic gadgets take up most of your time? The easiest thing, before you throw out your computer, is to practice, practice, and practice.

You know, some people say you can never predict what's going to happen five minutes from now. Maybe you can. Once, a long time ago I practiced something similar. You should try it also! It goes too well for me now!

# Thirteenth Chapter

I was in a so–called research laboratory, where an about one thousand pieced photo catalogue of landscapes and buildings were being showed to me. I could only see the cover of the catalogue, from the pictures in it not even one! Then they asked me to go into another room with a few empty papers and a lot of colourful pencils. Sit down, and five minutes later imagine five pictures, which the computer chooses randomly out of the catalogue. It chooses five numbers, five serial numbers of the pictures. In those pictures there were mountains, churches, hurricanes, characteristic buildings, etc. So, counting from now, five minutes later five pictures will be shown to me. My job was to draw the specific shapes of the five pictures beforehand, or draw down the whole thing if I can imagine it. Job understood.

At the first few occasions it was hard. A had only a few hits. I asked for more time. While I was relaxed, I concentrated sometimes for even half an hour, then I gave a signal when I was ready. Three from five, later four from five was my number of hits. I went here once a week for half a year. One of the regional professors, who specialized in futurology, told me that this average is very rare. After three months I received a private CD disk and got an inside view on other interesting things. One of their colleagues developed a device that could measure the amount of energy flowing from the human body. I really liked this machinery. It couldn't get overcharged. From him I heard an interesting story, with which they confirmcd the truth of telepathy being present and used between animals. The experimented were 100 specimens of rats collected from the street. The road that they had to go through was a labyrinth with ten entrances. They got the rats started in groups of ten. They accomplished their goal, which was the cheese, under the same amount of time. It was predicted that the last group of rats launched would reach the cheese under a shorter time, compared to the group which was launched first. How did they know the shortest way in the labyrinth? Because that distance was covered! They didn't have to go to any private course.

Us people go to private courses to get to know where our little cheese is, our money.

I was thinking of all this while I wasn't sure if I could stand up? I concentrated on my first chakra, the first from the seven, of which my bones are in the most connected relationship in. I saw that it is spinning slower. Operating in safe mode, just like Windows XP! But I felt that it was on standby. It needed some thoughts for help! I saw as I was eating more and more, my stomach working it up. My body delivers it with my blood into every cell; therefore my blood circulation will get faster. My heart beating faster! The blood is circulating faster in me. I started getting up slowly. I was still grabbing on the doorknob with both my hands, then pulling myself up higher and higher, I got to stand up. You can always rise up, even alone! True, it's easier with help. Many times only you think what a world–shaking problem you have! You can be sure that someone else has also had something similar.

# Fourteenth Chapter

I also have one in these days. My wife moved away from me. Took my two kids also. She got to know a man full of promises on the internet. Of course out of the promises nothing happened. My children cried many nights for me. The new guy is an occasional narcotic. Maybe slowly I'll get to the point, till the court doesn't bring a decision, that „I have to buy my own kids" if I want to see them. It's like my ex–wife has gone crazy. Neither of them work. They blackmail me by saying, that I can only take my kids away every two weeks for a few hours, if I pay them the discussed price! What would you do?

I think they would spend the money on narcotics! They're living in a dream world for a few months now and my two children are suffering for this! They say they are happy. Narcotic grown–ups. In these conditions what will happen to my children? Their school marks dropped a whole grade. They can't pay attention to the teacher properly in class. She even asked me what happened to them.

– I don't know – I replied. – I think the change of environment is the reason of everything. I asked the teacher to try to motivate the kids, by making them learn for me, their dad, who will always love them. It's not my fault that my precious wife fell in love. It will fade away anyway, like everything.

– I understand – said the teacher, then she added:

– I'm divorced also, in our case my husband found a new love, who I couldn't stand. The kids suffered because of this also. Many say that you should get divorced in a civilized way, but you can't. There's going to be some rage in it. Depends on your temperament. Unfortunately, I have heard about a husband taking her wife out in the forest at night, after he punched her on the face several times with clenched fists, there he pointed a gun to her head. That's how he asked her for them to stay together. Unfortunately, I understand. If there are kids also, at least because of them the problems should be solved quietly, keeping the things away, who doesn't see, etc. Then later things will turn out right.

    – Yes, that's true. My son is now ten years old. In front of his mother he told me, he can barely wait to come of age and then anywhere I'll be, he'll find me and come to me! My daughter then immediately replied that "I'm going also"!

    – Dear father! If you all can solve the problem, for them to study well, we hope everything will be fine. Excuse me, but now I have to go to class!

    – Thanks for your time, miss, best wishes – I bid farewell.


Was born in nineteen–ninety–seven
But had many dreadful things that happened.
My studies have gone wicked,
With scolding I've been rewarded.

But I am brainy,
Will even study,
I'll learn my tutoring,
And also all the poetry.

This is just a voluntary task, not else.
Just a poem in which my heart opens,
I mean, not my heart opens,
But my mind that comprehends.

This rhyme is not ending,
With it, have to practice spelling.
Till that this tidy poem is over,
But wait, later on there will be a poem bit rawer.

# Fifteenth Chapter

## Altered state of consciousness

From our infancy we involuntarily live through altered states of consciousness. In our life we exist in many conditions! As a child we let our parents know our needs by crying. I'm hungry, mom, I've done poo, change my diaper, etc. Later we indicate our needs by talking. Although many times, in a tighter child–parent relationship, you can notice that the parents sense what their children want as it were telepathy. Later on this connection can still remain in some kind of level. The increased usage of this usually can be observed between twins. One sibling can sense from far away if something good or bad is happening to the other one in that concrete moment. This ability we start to neglect inversely proportional as we learn how to talk. However, this is an extremely important ability built into, or instead, burnt into us, which isn't the same as previously assumed. As previous assuming I mean, when I think something about a person who is unfamiliar to me, without not having any exact information in that current matter. E.g., maybe he's bisexual. The truth is that he is not; I just thought that because of his clothing. He has a wife and children. But I only got to know these after I got to know him. I tried to catch the signals telepathically, but sadly my satellite antenna doesn't catch the signals in that frequency. You know, like telephones. 900, 1800, 1900 MHz exists. Besides those, the internet's parabola antenna works on 24420 MHz's.

What kind of device do I have for it? What signal do I catch? You know, what exists in material, as system, that exists in the level of soul also. In a SOUL level the improvement of a system is a little more time, because you have to consider the level of the transmission distance. As all telecommunication systems are continuously developed, it is absolutely important for me to improve my accessibility, as my given ability allows me to, to the highest level. So I have to go into a store to buy a cell phone, or have to get a subscription contract. YES! IN THE MATERIAL WORLD!

# Sixteenth Chapter

Once I worked with a colleague in a city totally unfamiliar to us. As we arrived, our boss showed us our accommodation and the closest big shopping mall, for us to buy some food there. After a month passed by, we knew all the products and started getting bored of the stores supply. We both were doing hard physical work; therefore we needed a big amount of calories. We worked in a four floor house; we had to go up and down minimum forty–fifty times daily, with some kind of tools or materials, on the stairs. Our feet by the end of the day asked permission to the bed nearly by their own, no need for sleeping pills. From the neighbours we got to know that this chain of stores has a bigger store at the edge of the city, next to an entirely new residential district. We both decided that because of the big distance we will visit it on Sunday. We set off at nine in the morning. We didn't know which way to go; didn't even know where exactly the new residential district is. I told my colleague, trust me, we will find it. Outwards from the city on one of the main roads we turned left, a little after the first traffic circle. We saw a completely bare field land. It was about four–five hectares. Through that there was a footpath, which took us to a stone–wall, which had a little gate. As we opened this we saw the new residential district! We went further for about ten minutes at the side of the stone–wall. Then another wall appeared at our left–hand sides.

My colleague then asked:

– Are we going the right way? We are walking for one hour now uselessly!

– Yes.

– From how do you know?

– I dreamt of it!

– Yeah, sure. I'm going to be very mad if we are wandering for hours because of your stupid dream, you can be sure in that!

– Look – I said. Do you see at our left that big, tall hall building covered with aluminum?

– Where?

– Here, about two hundred meters from here.

– Yes, I do.

– Well, we're going there.

– I don't believe you.

– Not a problem. Then let's bet! If that isn't that shopping centre, then I pay your shopping. If it is that one, then you pay mine!

– Good. But there should be an amount limit!

– Okay. 50 Euros. That's not that much!

– Fine!

A rock wall surrounded the building. As we turned to the road leading us there, and my colleague sighted the sign of the building, he said:

– I think I lost!

– It's okay. I'll dream further for you. But I'll have a very good day today! You pay my bill. I never even thought of this in my dreams! Oh, yes, how are you?

– Fine! At last we'll buy a big amount of meat as a calorie bomb! I want some bacon also, because I love it. And everything else! – He replied.

I probably looked around at night. Using the ability of my astral body I found the shortest way from our accommodation to the hypermarket. That's why we were able to go there straight away, without making any detours.

## Seventeenth Chapter

We deliver communication vibes towards the outer world. To the material, as to the astral worlds. This is a very important thing.

– Peace be in your heart! – told me a security guard, who claimed himself as a Buddhist.

Communication based on peace is the most important in the worlds, be it your enemies or your friends.

At a few animal shelters, where the so said tender working there, with different kind of objects – sticks, chains – beats up the animals, it's noticeable that the animals memorize the person and also the object which is hurting them. For them after this, the person who gets near them will arise the impression of the next beating. The animal already starts to get afraid when the person is only getting near them. Then it could be weird for the animal that after it is let out of the cage, I pet it for a long time with the stick held in one of my hands. If I repeat this more times, it will remember my scent. Maybe later, after a few days it will even accept some food from me. I can find its soul in a telepathic way with these thoughts: I am your friend; there is no need of a stick! I know that your teeth are stronger, but I want to be your friend! Depending on the amount of shock, more or less time is needed for an animal that came from a shelter to rehabilitate.

Can we imagine this? Can it be true that what we imagine with our own mind exits somewhere in the world universe on some kind of plane of existence? All the monsters exist somewhere from the movie Alien and even Godzilla! I think what exists in human mind in this world maybe exists in some kind of form on one of the planes of existence.

Can a human body be exchanged? Or a human body exchanges its soul? Is it imaginable? Then it can happen! The exchange happens through the top of the head; here we can step out of ourselves, after our helpers, protecting our silver cord, without doing any damage, create the exchange of the silver cords through our new and old body. The silver cord looks mostly like the thick, white coloured, flexible tube that came from the space suit of soviet astronauts and connected them to the spaceship. One cord coming from the astral world can tell us much about its owner.

## Medical coma

Sometimes in the television we can see people who fell into coma after suffering a severe accident. What happened? What can us, family members do? We can watch as they keep their body alive with machines. If we're lucky, then maybe they'll squeeze the hand set in theirs, or blink once–once. It's a dreadful torment to see one of your relatives on the bed, for years keeping them alive with in and out coming tubes from machines. Much patience is needed. The tiny signals captured by one of the family members can give the reason to hope, likewise to be sad. It's a painfully overwhelming period! Months, years of uncertainty come and we can't do anything. What happened? Why exactly that person? I think everything has a material and an astral explanation. The material accident affects those kinds of nerve regions that scared the soul of the person who suffered it, and as an escape they thought, they'll step out of their body, because they have done this many times in their dreams. The gate–keeper of the unconsciousness didn't find their spiritual self developed enough for their material self to get informed of the travels that were done in an unconscious state. They weren't properly prepared for this shock effect that stepping out of the body accidently would visualize the normal conscious self this experience as a traumatic event. The unconscious gate–keeper with this act protected the normal consciousness from the possible deep affect that would result as a negative experience.

The gate–keeper did a good job! The soul of the ill person wanders somewhere in between the astral planes, doesn't have any knowledge of that world, because the conscious self didn't get any information, thanks to the gate–keeper, who acted like this for their interest. Wandering around in a huge–huge world, in a world–mass made up of millions of worlds, where they look behind their back, they see their own silver cord, but don't know what it is. Their eyesight is restrained also. They aren't completely blind, only partially, since their third eye didn't open to sense the auras. They are wandering as if they would have left their horse at the edge of the forest and in a huge jungle, and was looking for the road leading back blindly. What are their chances? Would you follow somebody into a forest blind, to find and bring them back? How would you start? You know, there are guides everywhere, but everywhere you have to pay with something for it! What kind of payment could be asked from a blind person? With what could a blind person pay to a forest guide, to be taken back to the horse? Will the blind person find a guide on the way home? How many years till they get back?

Let's assume somebody else wants to get into this body and go on living this life. Coming back from the many years of coma, the family members experience with a shock that the person is partially amnesiac and doesn't even remember their names. Doesn't recognize anything; the house where they lived in is unfamiliar to them. They have to be reminded of everything as if they were not even themselves. The new soul in the body – just as my reincarnated dog – gets to know slowly the new environment. Has a difficulty getting used to the new job, what his or her education entitles them to do. The family and the environment recognize this also, and they show a big patience towards them. This is not true in every case. The body does not always change consciousness! Sometimes it just gets lost and a guide is needed. Somebody can wander for years between the planes of existence. The computation of time is totally different there! Unimaginable numbers of roads exist and even more options of choice to return back to the body. The problem actually rises from the lack of information. Our normal consciousness knows that if I sit into my car, which is the fastest way to my workplace, whereas that is the daily routine. If people would travel the same way in the astral world, with the possession of more information, these kinds of paths would be much shorter and purposeful. Unfortunately, many improvable abilities could be missing from somebody who involuntarily stepped out of his or her own body. As a child many abilities don't improve further for some kind of reason.

However, everything can be taught and learned! Mathematics can be aura sensing. Grammar can be telepathy, etc. We could likewise call the reducing and enlargement of objects, telepathy, hypnosis, astral body investigation, levitation, etc. subjects of the astral plane. The mine of abilities and skills are unlimited! We are also equally unlimited. Unlimited and the abilities we obtain even on astral level are immeasurable with any kind of human, material device. Similarly as the christen God JESUS!? The heavenly FATHER created us humans in his image – we can read. If we believe this, then we will have to believe the unlimited abilities of our own selves, which cannot be restrained by anybody else, just with our own choice by some kind of reason. There can be many causes to restrain certain ability, e.g., if the incentive to live isn't the same as the things intended ahead. A barrier can protect me! Sometimes I want to get somewhere faster, but our cars can only reach the speed of 190 km/h. Unfortunately the tyres of my car are maximized also for that speed. I, however, would like to speed with at least 230 km/h! I can't! Why? It's regulated for my own interest! I didn't do it, but the workers in the car factory did it for me, hereby protecting me from car crashing, accidents happening because of big speed. The speed of many new high–performance motorbikes is also limited. The competitors, who are on the road struggling for the first place, can get the devices that are the most suitable for them. Everybody according to their own abilities!

# Eighteenth Chapter

I'm sitting in my armchair. Thinking about my kids. I don't know how they are. I saw them last time in the morning in front of the school entrance, they were late again. I talked to their teacher, who said they are often late and their average study achievement is dropping. I don't know what to do. I just think about the things I hear, that they don't have any money, maybe just for narcotics, yet for that always. When I see my ex–wife she walks unstable. She doesn't go in a strait line, she staggers a bit right–left. She shoots herself during the daytime also, her neighbours said. I've been very nervous for months. I've thought about it many times that I go over to their house with an axe in my hand, while the kids are still at school, and smash the front door to pieces. Then I hit the knees of that narcotic sleazebag! If I could only know why was he born?! I think his mother gave birth to him crying–blubbering, while in big pain, because she could barely wait for that big piece of shit to come out of her at last! If the tram doesn't cut shorts on him, then I'll do it with an axe! I'll make him sit down on the floor, and I'll hit him on the knee, as a butcher does with the boney meat, till his thigh doesn't rip apart from his knee! Let his blood flow! Why did he have to tear apart a family with two kids!? Because he's the narcotic promise–man?! He promised my wife everything. I took it well that for weeks she slept one day at home, one day at this sleazebag motherfucker in turns! And I should be patient?! Although, she didn't arrive home in time not even then, many times only in the afternoon? Even when she was at home, she was walking around in the house with a telephone and headset on her head! She didn't even talk to me, because all the time she was in a telephone connection with that narcotic boy! The blonde, blue eyed dream guy! After the dye wearied out of his hair, it turned out that he actually has ugly red hair. He had a disgusting piercing in his eyebrow, which he later took out. However, at its place stayed a horribly hideous scar. Ugly, black scar! He's always wearing long sleeved hooded sweatshirts; under that the marks on both his arms of the needle pricked into his veins can't be seen. He shuttered apart my calm family life; he tore my kids away from me! I'll shutter his legs apart in exchange. I hope he won't be dazed, after a break in the door! I'm sure I'm going to hit his legs first! Let him collapse to the floor! I'll wait till he gets pale, then I'll talk to him. If he starts shouting, then I'll give one–two on his head also, but not too big ones. I want him to live for a few other minutes! I want to ask him a few questions. Is he Christian? If yes, then why did he sin against the Ten Commandments? What kind of punishment does he think, he will get after he tore apart a family? Why did he lie in such things that he had nothing to do with? Why does he want to be the father of unknown children? Why does he send my ex–wife to borrow money, for him to buy some drugs? He takes the kids to school, after he gets home with the junk; they shoot up their selves together.

I can't take it anymore! I have to stand up from my armchair! Where's the axe? In the garage. That's great, the car is there also! I go down the stairs. Open the door on the left in the garage. Switch on the light. My eyes are searching for the tool shclf. I see it, the axe in its place. Hung up, sharpened. I always put everything away sharp.

Now I really understand why! I'll kill this filthy son of a bitch! I run to the shelf. Get my hands on the axe. A very good, easy tool! Long edge, short handle.

With this I'll kill you, you pig! I turn. Behind me there's the car, through the windshield I see the ignition key and garage opener in it. I go around the front of the car. Open the door. Get in, start the car. I'm able to get out of the garage straight to the street; my neighbour didn't block the driveway. I look into the mirror, behind me nobody's coming. Clutch, first, pedal to the metal. I'll be right there. Red traffic light at the crossing. I look left–right, nowhere a car. Let's go further! I only want to stop at their house. I look at the seat on my side. The axe is there. The edge of it is shining, as the sun catches it through the windshield. I can barely wait to get into the house! I'll start with his legs, so he won't be able to run away! If he shouts, then I'll hit him with the back of the axe. Not with its edge, I don't want to kill him straight away. Let him get what I want to say, and let him have awful pains during it! He won't have bigger pain than mine! He tore my family away! Disgusting worm! He deserves worse! I will cut him into pieces! Until every piece of him isn't as least ten centimetres!

I'm here at last. The door is open. I step in. Somebody's coming towards me. I can't see clearly, its half–light. I hear the voice of a man.

– Hey, who's there?

I strike with my right hand three times. The point of impact of the edge of the axe is getting lower and lower. Perfect. I kick the door behind me in with my leg. It closed. No sound. Somebody is lying collapsed on the floor in front of me. All right, till now everything's fine.

95

Where's the switch? I hope no one is here! With my left hand I'm groping on the wall next to the door. Square shaped plastic. This will be the switch. It's set up upside down. I turn it on. Light flares up. I look towards the form. I've got you, you druggie sleazebag. I was too fast. I struck three times. One got his left shoulder. His shoulder bone is broke. He got a hit on his skull above his left ear. It's bleeding hardly. His face is also very bloody. You deserve it! Know I like you! If I'm lucky, they won't cremate you.

The body that carries these rotten thoughts will be eaten by maggots in your coffin! You were a disgusting worm! A hit above the wrist of the left hand. Blood is spilling from there too. My dad always said, your tools should always be sharp, that way you can work easier. He was right. Older people should be respected for their experience!

The chopping can start! I have to cut him into pieces! I'll bag him and take him away. I won't give your bloody pieces to the worms in the ground! It's enough if I put you into a litterbag and throw you into a big metal trashcan! The blood is already a lot here. I have to clean! Where's my wife? I'll find her! Let this rot here further! At last it's a corpse!

This is what I wanted. The world does not need such a person! Now nobody can separate me from my children! Luckily they're in school now. Today afternoon I'll go to the school for them, sooner than their mother. I searched in every room, nobody's here. I have to clean up! This scumbag died too early! I couldn't tell him anything! Although, I did have a few things to say!

You're only a druggie trash now! I have to start

slicing him up, but not here at the entrance. I have to clean here a lot.

There's too much blood on the carpet. It's okay. I'll pick it up and burn it in the fireplace! Then I'll take this shit in the bathroom and cut him up in the bathtub. I'll put his pieces into black plastic bags. That will be nice! I have to get started. He isn't more than seventy kilograms. At last he's dead! I have to pull a nylon bag on his head and upper body, maybe that way he won't bleed on the carpet that much. Done with that! He's in the tub. It was hard to pull him here. Where's my wallpaper cutting knife? In the left pocket of my jeans. Very good! Next to the wall I'll cut up the carpet, then till extension I can rip it of the floor with my hands. His blood is still fresh. Not much came out of him. But the bathtub is already bloody everywhere. It doesn't clot too fast. It's okay, let as much blood flow from it as needed!  I'll wait a bit, then I'll start to slice him up. Hands, elbows, shoulders. Feet, till knees, thighs. How many parts should I cut the upper body in? I'll see how it works out. Let's start! I'm very pleased. This creep is lying in front of me dead! Popped out eyes, head tilt to one side. Clearly bloody face. Red haired, blue–eyed corpse. See, I promised you something also, when you threatened me that you'll get me killed if I don't leave you guys alone! Now you're the CORPSE, not ME! You're lying here, you shame of humanity! I respect the Ten Commandments!

Till now! Now I sinned, but you did it sooner. Now you paid for eternity, no further! I still have an hour work with you, then everything will be okay. I'll fix the door lock, there nobody will come in! For days nobody will look for you. Till then I'll take my wife and children far away from this rotten city. I hate everything here! I hate internet also, that's where they get to know each other!

Okay, I've got the hands. Packed. Now the legs come. It's good that I brought the chopping–board in the tub from the kitchen. I'm holding the board with one hand. Okay, now comes the feet! This is simple here, at the bottom of the tub. I'll put his feet on this. Don't move it! Oh, you aren't moving it anymore... At last I get a grab on it. Right hand, axe, strike! Great! This is ready! Nylon bag. I'll be ready soon. Already have both of his feet in it. Lucky he was in slippers. This won't buy anymore shoes in the store from now on.

– Where are you?

– In my armchair.

– Are these your thoughts?

– Yes.

– Then let them go!

– You know, this has come to my mind several times. This line of thought always returns that I go over to his place and cut up that louse.

– I understand your rage. Your anger is right, it has a good purpose, but the fulfillment and the action are wrong. Look for another method to solve the problem! If the solution for you is getting back your family, your wife and children, then this is good! But that you want to slice up a person, that isn't good for anybody. If the cops catch you, maybe you'll never get out of the jail. You do more wrong for your kids with this than right. You could become a killer. But if that is what you want?! Think it through! You know, these are also your thoughts, they are coming from you! The highest purpose of them is good, but the method is very problematic. You have to find another solution! Wait for a while, ask for time! Later you'll have more information about everything! Maybe you'll see through things better! With time you'll have to choose from several things the right way! Murder is not a solution. It's imaginable that with time, we'll be able to help you too, but respect this part of yourself, because this is within you also. He gave you the first answer to the problem. He is a very useful factor of your pieces. He also has many other good qualities. Thank him for that suggestion to get to the solution! You will stay in touch with him the same way further on. You are searching for a solution that is acceptable and optimal for all of your pieces! Get help! We will help you! We all will support you here, trust us! In the last days, when you all were still living together, your wife shaved your head bald. You told her, you want her to do this, because you want to point out: you feel you have some defects, because of her leaving you. But I'll tell you something. By the time your hair grows to its normal length, you will already have your family back. You all will be together again. Believe it! Till then rest. Don't stop paying attention to your thoughts! Keep yourself occupied. Work therapy is a really good method. You like to work with quality, in a nice way. You approach every work with this attitude. Wood, stone, iron, water. You can meditate through all elements and feel them. You even work with this knowledge. You think, correct me if I'm not right, that after all, aether is the basic component of all elements, even of your body, with which you work by the help of your hands, and since you also live in that material, you are a part of it, as a part of the universe, therefore all elements are your friends! It is easy to work with it! Wake up, look around! One day it will be figured out!

– Yes, true, these are my murderous thoughts!

– If you killed him, you would step back one or more in the circulation of birth. He will surely suffer, because he has committed a sin. As the Christian Ten Commandments says, this is not only against the law of other religions and the circle of life what he has done, but it is also DESTRUCTION! A SIN AGAINST LIFE! This is punished everywhere! Even on the astral planes! We will help you. You know, you have friends here also, in the spirit world. They are those who haven't arrived to the astral plane yet, so they are floating in between earthly existence and astral existence. Those, who sometimes close doors and move objects, from what the normal person, using the ghost expression, gets frightened. They are no more than shadow creatures, who want to get attention by doing so. This is like, when someone sets off in an elevator and it stops in between two floors. He can't go down, and neither upwards – he is stuck inside the elevator! He can't go anywhere. He is pushing the alarm bell, but the person he needs to talk to is too far away, and has no time to care about him. He tries to move and object; maybe someone will notice and help him to get one existence level higher, because this is the goal. This is the most important, and in the society of souls, improvement goes mostly upwards in percentage. That few percent, which doesn't get higher, must do penance for their ugly sins. They roam in that level of their life, till they don't learn all the prescribed tasks successfully. What do you think, what should you learn out of this situation?

– Patience.

– Yes, and a lot of tolerance – Told me the gate–keeper of my unconsciousness.

– I see you started meditating. Finish it, I plead you. Wake up and go, take a shower. You have to be fresh! Unfortunately, tonight we have to attend a funeral. There it is daytime now. Get yourself together, they just informed me. Then lay down! We are travelling eight thousand kilometres on astral plane; it will be a very long trip. Be prepared, because if by that time your thinking baskets aren't empty, I'll have to leave you here, then you can't come with us.

We went to Tibet that night. We arrived to the entrance of a cave several thousand meters high. With many of my partners travelling in the form of a light sphere, we were rapidly moving inside the labyrinth. Only the one going in the front knew the exact path, he told us beforehand that we should follow only him, do not change our course in either direction. As getting deeper in the cave, there were a few torches, this way the dead–carriers saw better. The four of them brought the covered body through another entrance of the cave. They stepped slowly; you could see the great sadness on their faces. They were wearing the simplest votary dress. I saw many companions, who were similar to us, travelling also like astral balls. We were gathering. They took the body into a big chamber. He passed away not long ago, we all knew him: he was one of our greatest teachers. He was very old. We unravelled ourselves from our ball form and started praying for his soul.

His soul will not be reborn again; he will become one with the aether of the immense universe. He got to that level in his lives, where he was only viewing things, and at the same time his soul was imaginated, over many decades and many previous lives, with the instrument of meditation into every living or inanimate objects and beings. HIS SOUL WAS IN EVERYTHING AND HE WAS IN EVERYTHING ALSO! Now it will fulfill: he becomes one with the aether, the universe. The life cycle spins on and on. Like a drop of water in the ocean, that's how his soul pours apart in the immense universe. Then somewhere, if someone is in need of this drop, he will find it. Then the cycle of his soul starts again, existing further on material level. Everybody knows that for life, water is needed, without it there is only death. Water keeps everything alive.

Many of us murmured the same pray in chorus. The light of our astral bodies was shinning stronger in the light of the torches, which were placed in the cases on the wall. The ceremony was held for a few hours. On the way back I asked my unconsciousness where I got to know this great lama from. Thereupon, he showed me some fragments from the end of my previous life. Around the Indian and Tibetan border I was driving a motorbike with a side–car. In the side–car this lama was travelling with me. We had to escape from the monastery. I knocked out a Chinese soldier for this motorbike; I didn't have any other choice. He wanted to kill me, as they done to all our other mates. We were travelling very fast, on a forest path. We arrived to a tall railway embankment, under it was a small tunnel, through there led our way further, but we didn't get there. On the two sides of the tunnel there were plaque signs with English language text on it. Unfortunately, with a motorbike you can't travel without making any sounds. We were about fifty meters from the entrance of the tunnel, when a train pulled by a locomotive passed through the railway. I slowed down. The sound of the motorbike was louder than the train, so I only recognized later that it was coming. From the window of one of the trucks, an army clothed arm reached out and he threw something towards us. It exploded next to us. It was a hand–grenade! Our vehicle turned over, caught into flames! I fainted. I saw my body on astral plane; many fragments of the bombshell caught me. The gasoline tank in front of my stomach later exploded. I luckily tumbled down on to the side of the embankment a few seconds before the explosion. I was lying on the side of the embankment, in a Chinese uniform. I took it off the guard after I knocked him out. His faded clothes now on my body got improved with a few bombshell holes.

I was lying on the side of the embankment and I didn't feel pain. We had to escape; otherwise our earthly life would have ended by the Chinese soldiers. Who we buried was the same as who just escaped, he didn't get harmed, only fell out of the side–car. In that second his life was more important than mine. In my present life, after this incident, I understood why I am so repulsive toward riding a motorcycle. The train rolled onward, only the uprising, thinning smoke indicated that it recently passed. I woke up in an underground sick–ward, although I didn't want to. My body was in a really bad condition. The doctors didn't pay attention to the uniform on me; they treated me as a critically ill patient. They took a lot of pieces of lead out of me, then I got infusion for weeks, that was what kept me alive. After I was lying in coma for weeks many gave up on me. In astral plane we talked a lot about my previous life. The doctors did everything they could that was possible back then. I gave up on my body, barely had any pulse. I saw myself lying in the bed from above. I had to think it through, should I wake up at all? One of the nurses tended me with big attention, as if I were alive. She bathed me on my bed, cleaned me, changed my sheets. The other patients and doctors were also bothered by, in their opinion, the too big attention. She sat at my bed many times, whilst holding my hand. Till that, she talked in herself to me. She really wanted me to open my eyes. She was attached to a stranger! She treated me as my living ill fellows: she dressed, bathed, moved my body parts, for me not to get anaesthesia. I felt it, I knew, she really wanted me to wake up. People unknown for me were lying on the other beds, but they saw how the nurse made an exception with me, and some looked at me with envy. She received offensive words.

– Why are you caring about a living dead? He hasn't woken up for weeks now; the infusion is a waste on him! – told her the man who was lying on the bed next to me. He broke his leg. He was lying with his leg secured by a splint, but he could walk with a crutch.

Yet, the nurse tended me very persistent and hard–working, in the belief that once I would come back and open my eyes. This caring touched me. I started to get to like her and I didn't want to disappoint her. One night, when everybody was already sleeping in the sick–ward, Nurse Rita was sitting next to my bed tired. She was holding my hand with both of her hands, her upper body and head was on the edge of my bed that was how she was sleeping. After waking up, she stayed there, looking at my closed eyes for hours, waiting, if I would open them. Then she doze off again.

Only lesser or greater snorts and breathing were audible. Maybe everybody was in a deep sleep. I had to get back into my body, and thank her for her faith and the caring of me. I was thinking about this. The time had come.

After my body felt sensible to me, I slowly moved my free hand, then slowly, moving only my fingertip, I gradually squeezed her hand. I opened my eyes. Looked at her. She slowly woke up, sat up. I saw the amazement on her face. She was still holding my hand. Emotion overcame her as she looked at my face. A little teardrop came into the corner of her eye. I slowly started talking. I thanked her for all her efforts. I promised her, we would meet again, but now I had to die in this body. The significance of me dying was for the high positioned abbot to escape from the certain death waiting upon him. Nurse Rita didn't understand anything. I told her then a few things about death, rebirth, and the different worlds. She was listening in silence. She didn't ask, didn't interrupt me. I write this down difficultly. I can't put this into words clearly; many emotions are whirling inside me now. I recalled the last time I died, with this saving my master, whose funeral I just attended. And here I met the soul of my present wife, for whom I later could barely wait to be born. I was waiting for her.

# Nineteenth Chapter

Sometimes I thought, made up some kind of new thing, method or procedure. But in many cases I must admit: I have never done something that hasn't been previously done by someone. Maybe the only difference is that I look upon the subject matter in another connection, with another approach. This is like brain research. There are some researches that say, the brain can also be compared to the sheet of a chequered mathematics notebook. The chequers between the corner points store the information, the lines are the paths, on which the answers arrive for the questions raised. This path isn't always the shortest; there may be many detours on the way that can extend the information until we say it to somebody. On the chequered paper, many variations can happen on the information lines. The corner points can also have the transmitter role, and they can also be in a diagonal way. Which one is faster? In our everyday, routine–like done tasks, we live with nearly automatically practiced moves from the up drawing of the task, till the accomplishment of it. E.g.: tooth–brushing. We don't even think through how many new and different experiences can be born then, and mean a new quality, when one–one old, everyday activity is done in another way.

I always admired those European football players, who can handle the ball with both legs equally.

For me my right foot is determinant in this game. The individual, who has an opportunity to drive not only a right–handed, but also a left–handed car and the other way around, can go through a smaller catharsis. Both are a frenetic experience at the beginning. One of these kinds of experiences for me was when I first drove into a double striped traffic circle, which for me was in the opposite driving direction till then.

Till this day, whenever I'm at a left sided traffic road that traffic sign jumps into my mind, which had this text: Keep right!

# Twentieth Chapter

We breathe every day. Our body is filled up with invigorating air, as well as the bodies of our fellow–beings. It passes through our blood vessels and sustains us. Everyone breathes in the air in a different rhythm; some do it slowly, others quickly. Usually when we are nervous our breathing is faster. The boxer fighter blows out the air the same time as he hits. At least this is taught to most of the boxers. The marksman retains his breath, and tries to stiffen before he pulls the trigger.

Lovers often breathe in the same rhythm, which reflects the harmony between them even in an unconscious way.

If our boss breathes nervously, gasping, or quickly, and talks to us angrily, the most annoying thing we can do is to behave exactly the opposite way, telling him calming words:

– Calm down, there's nothing wrong. I already know the solution to this problem. I'm going to handle it soon. When I'm finished I will inform you immediately, while doing this, set a smile from ear to ear on our face, and all our gestures show our confidence, since we really do know the solution. And what if we don't? Then we pretend that we actually do! There is nothing more to do only to gather further information to solve the task, evaluate them, and to carry it out as soon as possible with the most effective tool. Many bosses work off their temper on their secretaries if they don't know something. The lack of self confidence, which arises from the lack of communication with ourselves, always results in anger, fear and rage.

An example:

– Dear secretary, please remind me that this afternoon I'm going to have an important conference with the Mayor.

Instead:

Hey you, inside there, please tell me where I put my ignition key, my wallet, my calendar, etc. I ask you only because you are in me also, and we work in a team together–for each other. I help you and you help me!

The answer:

– All right, but you also should pay attention to all your work today! You can save a lot of time and mental energy, if you always put your things, you use in the everyday life, on the same place. Instead of dealing with your odds and ends your secretary would have more time for bigger projects, which she could handle independently and responsibly after a short time. But don't overload yourself either. There are things remembering instead of you as well, but your memory is the best! Indeed, in everyday life, the consciousness of all people operates on two levels. There's a conscious part, plus the big plus, the unconscious! While you work, your conscious part clearly sees what is in front of you, while your unconscious part spontaneously adds your experiences you gained throughout your life in this field. You hear the words, which are assessed as words by your unconscious part, and it compares them with your past and future actions. Your conscious part can consider some things important, but your unconscious pays attention to every, EVERY small detail. Your conscious self can listen in an altered state of consciousness to the things said, while your unconsciousness is in the most suitable trance, and remembers all the important things you need. Your conscious part might have forgotten what the essence of things is, but your unconscious part can remember back later. Meanwhile, important questions may arise, but mostly your unconscious already knows the answers. Your conscious part is still looking for solutions, while your unconscious already knows that processes of thoughts that have started in you, which will lead to an active solution. Your conscious part doesn't do anything new or anything exciting while your unconscious part does things that go well beyond curiosity.

Sometimes your conscious part is diverted, if it doesn't understand something, but your unconscious works quickly without any efforts, and can concentrate easily. When you first "argue" with yourself about something like whether to go somewhere or not, your inner selves appear. One of your parts says don't go. Both of them have their own reasons, which can be considered as good aims in their point of view. So, both of my parts may be equally important to me. For the first time when we realise this, it is more important that two of our parts are communicating with each other, and make their voices heard shrilly, than the argument itself. All of our selves have their good aims, from which the results are intended for us as a present in our life. The highest goals include: wisdom, peace, love, inner peace.

I'm not schizophrenic, and no one is! Merely many people don't communicate with their selves in the same quality. Some of them may be repressed, while others are given too much freedom. During our rebirths, several selves became a part of us, which needs to be integrated as a large, comprehensive whole, for the improvement of us, all our fellow human beings, and all of the creatures in the worlds. I think, being here now, that this is possible. Let's imagine it.

Let's make ourselves comfortable, relax and release all our thoughts! There are many recurring daily problems, which are waiting to be solved perfectly. Let's reassure our thoughts coming to the surface, and those who brought them out, so that later on we will solve these with even bigger attention, but right now please be a bit quiet, because we have to go to a large auditorium, where they are also warmly welcomed.

I am sitting or lying in a position which is best for me. My thoughts are clear. I'm in a large auditorium. I don't know how it looks like. For some people a usual one can be the one at universities, for others it means the theatre. I stand on a podium on the stage. In every row in front of me there is someone sitting there. They are scattered, and a large number is present. There are women and men as well. Their clothes show a large variety from the very tattered to the nicely dressed ones. They also varied in age. There are some kids, and I see some elderly people also. There are a lot of empty chairs. I look down from the podium, and speak into the microphone:

– I have this problem! Who wants, and who can help? – I cast my eyes over the auditorium in all directions. An elegant man of my age raises his hand in the first row. I let him speak, showing this with a movement of my arm. He stands up slowly, confidently, and says:

– You know, I've already told you this thing a thousand times! This shall be done like this! – And he explains my deeds endlessly, which I often did in these cases. But I have a feeling that I need something else now. I know, and I feel that his highest aim is good for me, but now I need something more. I thank his suggestion, and he sits back. I promise that I will consider it.

The things, he said, can be a correct guidance to me on a large scale, but I would be curious about other ways to achieve the goal, so I look at the room again. In the back, on the left side I see a hand lifting up, but someone the one who's sitting next to him, tries to pull down his arm. I realise this. I tell him:

– Hey, back there! Can you please leave that man! Please come closer so I can better hear what you want to say, because I probably wouldn't understand you clearly, you are so far away from me right now. Till now I haven't noticed you.

The answer:

– Yes, of course, you haven't even noticed nor heard me so far. Although, I was always here. Many times I could have helped you to reach your highest goals even faster, things like WISDOM, PATIENCE, HEALTH, LOVE.

– Hey you, next to me, let me go! Stop pulling me back all the time! – With a sudden movement he pulled his arm out from the gripping hands of one of my selves, sitting next to me.

– What do you want to say with this? Come here in front of me to see and hear you better! As I can see, your clothes are quite shabby, and you haven't been to the hairdresser for a long time either. What have you done lately? Where were you?

– I am one of your neglected selves YOU didn't take care about! You have never addressed me before, haven't asked my opinion either, although I always wanted the same things as the previous speaker!

– Then sit beside him in the first row, and we will all listen to your suggestion!

The solution was voted unanimously after a long debate. Then my two selves united, whereas their goals were the same now. Now an even better dressed part of me, wearing a more expensive suit, and shoes, stepped forward, my main, MAIN advisor! I often come to this room. I also had child aged parts of me, whose development stopped in my childhood. I brought them up, as I did with the others as well. They became mature big–boys, full of confidence, faith, love, and peace. I'm talking about all my mates, who are standing next to me, and during decades of communication they have become my innermost, most honest, devoted friends who always help me in trouble. But some people are standing behind them! I rarely meet them. Their got to know about their existence, when I was in one of the deepest trance, doing a three–hour–and–a–half–long practice with an English and a Hungarian psychiatrists.

I volunteered, because beforehand the steps of the practice were told me precisely. I was curious about the results.

The English psychiatrist, Peter, spoke English, which I understood somehow although previously I haven't studied this language before.

Meanwhile, I continuously heard Gabriel's words as well. They didn't tolerate each other! Deliberately, they talked to me constantly all the time. They asked me what I was seeing. They talked to me from two sides continuously without interruption. In the meantime I was communicating with my inner parts, and told them the answers my inner parts said to their questions. Till that time the number of my selves decreased, only twenty–thirty remained. Over the time, many of my selves had recognized their common goals, and became one with each other.

The practice was successful. Both doctors were pleased. At the end they asked me if there was still something I would like to say?

– Yes.

– What is it?

– Now that I looked behind me, I noticed three figures inside of me, with whom I haven't managed to communicate yet, I only see them.

– All right. This is your inner world, no one else's. What do you see them like? I ask this, because till now your selves appeared to you as perfect gentlemen, who are always helpful. Who are your new creatures? What do you think about them?

– Three figures. A woman and a man, they're holding each other's hands. They are as tall as me, and equal to me. They are happy that we met. They always watched my actions from behind. We are all delighted by the fact that we met. VERY MUCH! I think one of them is my female part; she wears a beautiful oriental dress. The man is my male part. He is such a thoroughly honest gentleman, what anyone would want to be. Now I can easily talk about anything with them – I said.

– And who is the third one? – They asked.

– The third one? He is about four meters high, standing behind the man and the woman. He has long hair, might be some kind of god. He has a large white cloak on his shoulders. He is my age. I can't speak to him. He speaks to me, I feel like I should listen to him. He says:

– You must do what we already designated for you! You must go on this road. You can make detours to the right and left, but you will waste your time unnecessarily, sooner or later you will return to me like everyone else! Put away the memory of this encounter, and continue to live as it is designated for you! We will meet later.

That's all he said. At the end of his arms, from the fingertips, golden threads led to the nicely dressed figures standing by my two sides in rows. I see this when I look left and right. I think he controls everything. I can't put it into words that exactly who he is, but I became pretty calm that I could see him, and he talked a few words. I suppose all the conversations are over.

– Well, then thank everyone for the creative cooperation. Tell them that everyone is equally important to you, you will continue to respect all of them, and you will still love them the same way you did!

– I guess we can finish the practice.

– What kind of experience did you have? Positive or negative?

# Twenty–first Chapter

I think that I can only do a certain ACTS under certain CIRCUMSTANCES, because I'm only CAPABLE of it here. I guess that it gives me some kind of HIGHER PLUS and only with this plus can my life be more complete.

Many people smoke, and maybe even more want to quit. It is kind of a social activity as well, which may even lead to new acquaintances in a certain atmosphere. For example, I ask for some light with a cigarette in my hand from a person who seems sympathetic. At work, and other places, it is possible to get to know people in this form as well. In some European countries a very good method has been used to make people break the habit, which is, smoking is prohibited in restaurants and pubs. If someone wants to fill their lungs with flavoured smoke, they have to go outside in front of the entrance. It is like the other people inside the building would have chased the smokers out.

– What did I miss? – They may ask when they come back. – Maybe a good joke or something else?

They miss something for sure. After that they start to feel shut out from the society, in spite of the fact that they may have had started smoking beforehand to show that they belonged to this circle.

It's all the same with drugs and alcohol. People are somehow looking for companions who don't always criticise them (e.g.: in family surroundings), but accept them the way they are. However, later on people take advantage of them imperceptibly. The first step is that they change their environment without attracting much attention. After this, absolutely new behaviours emerge, since maybe at home the parent opens the door on their child and asks:

– What are you doing?

In other places no one asks anything, but: Do you want more dope? Then pay for it!

But you don't have any money, since you're a student, Mummy's darling. The spending of pocket money starts, then minor thievery. First from the closest place, from the parents. After many quarrelling, the parents' trust slowly gets used up. But you need the money, because you have to shoot up yourself! Just out of plain stubbornness! It doesn't matter that I'm a student, I can buy it, and not only at weekends, but on weekdays as well. And I can stand harder drugs as well, because who, if not me? My friend tried everything also. He told me how good it is. The whole thing is an ecstasy! And if I only use it, maybe the police won't punish me so, just for a few days. I love this feeling, and I'd give everything to get it, always, whenever I want!

This became my life. I'm addicted! I rot here, in a dirty by–street, next to a large metal trash container. I am alone. I haven't eaten or drunk anything for two days. That's when I shot myself up last time. I can't stand up, my head hums, and I see things blurry. I see the picture of my mother, my brother, and my sister. Everything is chaotic! No problem, it will go away if I can get dope again. I just can't stand up! My feet have gone numb. What's happening? I don't understand. Maybe someone who passes by will help me. I see someone coming, almost here. I'll address him. Only about three more meters, and he is here. I open my mouth, but I can't speak only moan! What is this? What does he say!?

– Rotten junkie! Why are you lying next to the container? Why not inside of it? Sooner or later you will get there anyway! – He kicks me in the head with his boots, and I'm floored. I hear him laughing mockingly.

– Well this one didn't need much more! He may have already taken the running jump!

Maybe he has already dropped dead.

I thought there was only one man coming toward me, but there were two of them. I don't remember more.

I wake up in a room, sitting on a chair. I slowly open up my eyes and look around.

Everything is white around me. A man is coming towards me. He asks me who I am. I can't answer! He grabs my jaws with his left hand from behind and raises my head. He looks into my eyes.

– Who are you, what are you? I have been asking these questions for three days! You are awake, but you don't answer! I'll ask you again! Who are you, what are you?

Slowly something comes into my mind, but I'm afraid to tell him. All my parts are numb. I got some kind of medication. I take a distant look to my forearm; I see new marks of pin–pricks.

– I'm a doormat – I say softly. Nothing else came into my mind.

Another man's voice asks behind me:

– What did he say? Did I hear it well?

– Yes – answers the man in front of me. – He's a doormat!

– Ah, I see. That's very cool! IF you really are a doormat, then you can be kicked, bitten, and plucked, just like my puppy usually does it at home! I hear his voice behind me. He is coming closer and closer to me.

– Let's keep on kicking him – says the one in front of me.

– All right! This should be done.

– Kick it very strongly, until it falls off from the chair, if that's what he needs!

– He was fourth–year student at the university. An excellent student. He became a rotten druggie! And now a doormat! Can you get even deeper?

– I don't know, but let's give it to him!

Both of them started to kick me from both my sides. Pretty big ones. My legs, my thighs, my arms hurt. Now it's not numbing, it's HURTING. I put my hands in front of my face. I'm lying on the floor on my left side. In the meantime they are continuously kicking me, but it seems to me that there not doing it too strongly. The man standing behind me says:

– So, what are you then? A doormat or a human? Because I always kick doormats, but I love people very much! So, what are you? – He asks, and in the meantime he kicks my back even harder than before. I make a grab at it. Suddenly I straighten my back. My spine hurts.

– Okay, leave me! I'm a human! – I reply.

– What are you? I don't understand!

– Say it again – He shouts me in my ear – because I don't hear you! What are you? – He shouts even louder.

– Yeeeeees! I'm a human, a human! – I answer a bit doubtfully.

– Stop it! – He says to his partner. – This went pretty quickly. Finally he came to his senses! Come on; let's take him out of here! His parents are already waiting for their child. Let's show him to them! Finally he became a man!

They grab me from the two sides under my arms, and carry me out of the room. I can hardly walk. My legs are just hanging behind my torso. They carry me as a big piece of meat with consciousness. I see my mother, my father. My goodness! When did I see them last time?

Since I moved in to the university dorm, we barely met. Is it sure that they are my parents? As I'm coming closer I see their faces better. My father is wearing his old chequered jacket. Then they should be them. I remember, every time when they had to go to official places, my mother made my father wear this one. I'm here in front of them. I can't speak, I just keep silent. I think this is the best now. They surely know everything. But what? It doesn't matter. It's not that important now. I just won't say anything, that can't cause any problems. Strange questions. I don't answer.

– Are you okay, my son? Are you conscious?

I nod. Both of their faces are very desperate.

– Sure he's all right? – My father asks the doctor standing next to me.

– Oh, yes, he is absolutely all right, but we will have a lot of work with his consciousness. We have to carry him through many stairs. Now he is like – sorry for this expression – an industrial zombie, who has already got over a life–threatening drug overdose, but if he went home, he could relapse into this again. We shouldn't expose him to that risk. I suggest, if you all approve, that we take him back to his spiritual self with the help of a long therapy, while we make him aware of his identity. We would change the beliefs, which evolved in him after he got into the change, where he accomplished his aims in the environment he got into with the abilities he beholds. You know, he is one of the victims of drugs! He wanted to be happy, nothing more. We care for him, because it's worth doing it! You should sign some papers in my office. I'll meet you two in my office in a few minutes. Now, I'm sorry, but we have to take your son back to his room with my colleague. We will be back soon, some patience please. Is all understood?

– Ye–yes – replied my mother confused.

They drag me back to my room, push me on the bed. No one is here. White walls, white beds. They've just locked me up. I hear the knocks of retreating shoes. They're gone. I'm alone. But where am I? How did I get here, and since when have I been here? Did I really want to be happy? And perhaps relieved? Now I'm nothing but a sick druggie alone in a room. Was I ever really happy or relieved? No! It didn't give me the feeling I wanted. Only now the opposite one. At least my parents stand by me. Well, at least they didn't give up on me. I think my girlfriend – as I remember – maybe broke up with me? Yes! For sure! I'm not feeling fine! This isn't happiness! That's bullshit! In fact, I have my ass in an even bigger sling.

Did I learn anything at the university!? Maybe the doctor next to me, was talking about that to my mother? Studying is the relation between changes, and inner communication. I was always good in this, so how exactly is it? First: atmosphere, action, ability, belief, identity, and spirituality. Maybe I'm starting to come to my senses? Backwards all the levels organize the information of the one below it, and on every level we can alter something according to their rules. Changes on lower levels may have an effect on higher ones, but it's not inevitable. But changes on higher levels always alter the lower ones. There can be a lot of trouble from pieces of information mixing between levels. I had to cram this information. What's the point? Now I have time, and I will have plenty, to think about these things!

I wake up by the sound of the door lock. I might have slept a few hours. Although, I don't know the time, and neither if it's night or day. Two big white coated men enter the room. They close the door behind them. One of them hides both of his hands in his coat pockets, as if he's hiding something. I don't know what it is. I ask.

– Excuse me, doctor – I say but he interrupts me:

– Hey, look! Can he talk!? Unbelievable! We gave him so many sedatives that I thought he would never wake up again. It doesn't matter. We brought some again. – While he is talking, he slowly pulls out his hands from his pocket. In his palm there is a prepared hypodermic syringe. He tells his fellow:

– Ok, hold him down, don't let him move! I hate these hyperactive birds! What's up, mommy's favourite? Your mommy has a lot of money? It is very good because then her stupid kid can be here for a long–long time! Don't be afraid of me! I'll cure you from everything! You get injections for a few months. Everything will be fine! Well, pull your pyjamas sleeve up on your left arm! I don't have time! – He says obviously restlessly.

I don't like the look of him, he is lying, I can see it. His eyes tell everything. I also studied this at the university: average right–handed people look upwards to the right when they imagine something. When they hear the sounds of this image, they look right the same way, but the eyeballs are in the middle. When they are wandering on old stuff, they look to the left. Yes, and now he has the syringe in his left hand as well. I need to give in! The effect of this will pass too! I roll up my pyjama sleeve, and stretch my arm towards them. I do not know what is in the syringe; it can be venom as well.

– Good boy! Well done. You'll sleep soon, mommy's little favourite! – A malicious grin appears on his face. – Well, you see how clever you are! It wasn't a loss that you attended that expensive university! Others never earn throughout their whole lives as much money as one year of your tuition fee! –And well, well, we can greet you among the walls of this famous institution! Everyone is glad that you are here! Ok, we're done! – And with this he pushes the syringe into my vein. Good night, sweet dreams! Tomorrow we meet right here, just a bit earlier!

My vision starts to grow dim quickly. The medication is having an effect on me, I can feel it. I'll soon be asleep. What will happen to me? Am I going to wake up? I hope, I'll sleep.

In my dream, I'm wondering how many different realities exist. Was it a real happiness when I was rolling around shot up, in ecstasy in all kinds of places? What did I see? What did I hear? What did I feel? Was it good for me? It was! I learned too much. I learned a lot about communication and behaviour. And even though I still don't know what is reality! What is it? What I see, hear,

123

feel? Or what I hallucinate under the influence of drugs? Or the creatures of the astral world? What is real? Which one is real? I do not know! From where do the pictures come when I use drugs? From me! Only from me! There's nothing more but me! Nobody else! What happened with my inner parts? Didn't they want the same? My well–being? I remember when we attended this course, one of our fellows suddenly died. He had no medically traceable illness. Many of us thought that he pulled apart from inside. He didn't want to live! But what about me? Am I also going to pull apart and die? Who can help me? I don't know, I'm puzzled. I feel that many of my inner selves are fighting against each other. They are screaming, shouting to each other; instead of joining the energy that they use up for this. I hear a big, screaming chaos in me. They are shouting to each other in a terrible voice. Now my head started to hurt, I can't stand this too much longer! I have to escape from here! But from where? From my own body? If I leave my body, I will die! No, I don't want to die, but the cacophony is terrible! Who was I before? A successful student, a top class boy, an excellent student, a good athlete. They scream so much, I can't hear anything! I must end this!

Where shall I go? I feel like I'm moving away from my parts. It's not possible, I must turn back! Ok, let's stop now! Let's turn back! I open my mouth:

Everybody shut up! – I shout over the voices. – I said shut uuuuuuup! Fucking gosh! What the hell are you doing? What is this mess in me? How do you look like? And who are you? I don't know you!

– Oh, don't you recognize me? I'm your drug happiness! How do I look like? Do you like me?

In front of me I see a middle–aged, hollow–eyed, lame chap wearing tattered clothes and having a lack of teeth.

– Well, did you take a good look at me? Lately you loved me the best! What happened now? Where did you want to go just now? Did you want to flee away from me? Do you have dope in you now? I would like to project delirious pictures for you again! Would you like it as well?

– Sorry, there is nothing in me. I think I have to sit down and talk to everyone! Let's gather all of us together, and let's sit down in a circle next to each other as we used to do, and let's discuss everything. If someone wants to say something, raise your hand, and we give the word. Clear? I guess we have to look for other ways with and for each other to reach happiness, because forgive me, but the drug brought me to this psychiatric institution, and I will be glad if I ever manage to get out of here. The nurses keep on giving me sedatives and sleeping pills! We have to decide what is the true reality, and what is it good for? What is it that I need to see, and what is it that I don't?

One of my selves raises his hand high.

– I think you should see, hear and feel everything – he said. You know, if you don't want to hear something on purpose, your own inner selves will make you impaired of hearing or deaf for the sake of you. If you do not want to see something, you can become visually impaired or blind. You know it exactly what I'm talking about, as well as when you have such problems, you have to remember your first bad experience related to it. The first one, and from there you have to make the whole experience positive, so that you can undo your limits you built for your own protection. From that moment your physical problems will be solved as well! Your body's energy system and your chakras will operate as normal. Do you understand? I know you do, and as for me, I'm just repeating myself again and again. Get Started! – And with this he sat back, while the others nodded in approval.

# Twenty–second Chapter

I have been sleeping again, and deeply continuously for weeks now. Maybe as a reward, but I always get the next dose of sedatives or sleeping draught. The food is junk. They don't give me pills, because they think, I wouldn't swallow them. They give me injections. They push it well, deep into me, that's for sure! I have so many pin–pricks on my arms. Last time I got it into my bottom. I'm not able to lie on my back, only on my side. In the beginning I heard something about them starting some sort of therapy with me, but as I'm counting, I have been here for several weeks, and nothing happened. It's just plain madness! It's a complete nuthouse! They treat me like a narcotic or do they want me to go insane? Or do they just keep me in with sedatives and sleeping draughts, because my parents pay for my medication treatment anyway?

And what if they stop paying? They consider me cured, and suddenly put me out on the street? Are my parents even interested in me?

I haven't seen them for a long time. Perhaps they visited me here once, but I don't remember. So much time has passed by. Maybe my thoughts are clearer, because I get less sedative. I don't know, I don't know this either. But I know one thing; I want to break out from here. I have to go away from here; I have to regain my health.

No! I have to be healthy! It's going to be difficult to get out of here, but all aims can be divided into smaller details. Let's see! What is my aim? There's another thought here that is mine.

I remember a TV show, which was about eight–, ten–, fourteen–year–old African children. They were child soldiers, and for shooting down an enemy soldier they got some food, and drug as a reward! The leaders of the guerrilla group raped some of them, just for pleasure. It's an absolutely natural thing for them, they get no punishment! They are children separated from their families, who might have been sold by their own relatives to relieve the prolonged poverty for a short time. A team of children which kill for drugs in an organized way! By the time they grow up, they become human wrecks like me! I started it later. I didn't intend on it for a reward. I didn't have to kill while I was young, to be dazed and happy. No one lied to me that the other kids were my brothers, and my commanding officer was my father. I was not forced either. No one hit me, no one beat me up to kill, but I'm still here. I think I'm smarter than these children. Although, I'm older in age, I am not more intelligent than them. I'm not starving, I'm not freezing. I have a father, and a mother. I had a good life.

I started to blast with my friends. Then the harder ones came, and more. And there was nothing left just to steal and beg. Stolen stuff was given to pawnshops. And the money went to the pusher. And the dope into me. It was good. But I think there has been nothing for a long time. Maybe I feel better. At least I would like to. And I would like to get out of here, but not at all costs! I want to be considered cured and live with my family, and my girlfriend. Maybe she hasn't forgotten me. We loved each other very much, after the university we wanted to get married. Later on we would have had children as well.

We planned to have our own small family house, and many other things. Maybe it can still happen.

Which one is the illusion? The search for my own inner happiness, or the happiness I would like to reach with outer things? Exactly how old am I? Twenty–two. Wow, that's great! Let's check my calendar. I hope I can go through it precisely! Later on the next dose of sedatives may come. So, the first period lasts from one to seven. Everything is seven. Like there are seven days in a week, from week to week everything is seven. Seven is the winning number. Energy levels can be found on seven levels in our body, and we have seven main chakras. God created the world in seven days according to the Christian religion. I don't know if God's days lasted for twenty–four hours, and whether one hour lasted for sixty minutes? Or the basics of the calendar were something else that time?

I heard somewhere that all the deeds have their own glory. So seven times seven. I need to charge my batteries again so that I could work normally. After my body gets normal fuel, and I'm not narcotized with drugs! My heart is the engine; my kidneys, my spleen, my liver, my lung and other things are my accessories that are needed for moving. They can be replaced, but after that I would carry out the same activity very slowly. The new part need to recover again!

The first Seven: my bones inside me. Earth is the battery on which I am. The location of the centre: I'm just sitting on it. In which direction is it moving? The ones of women work in the different direction. Its colour: yellow. My snake slept here until it woke up, and climbed up higher and higher on my spine. It found its place on the top of my head. Its place has always been here. It quickly settled down into the most natural position. Its journey took a long time. How did it wake up? My attitude, to the world has changed, and I started to be motivated by earning more, and saving up money. I was chasing after unreachable aims, of which I knew deep inside that I would never be able to reach them, so after many disappointments, I returned from the pink clouds to the ground. After this I set up small, tiny goals for myself, from day to day. And when I managed to reach a small goal, possessing some newer and greater experiences, I started to plan the next small aim. And many little make a mickle! I'm in connection with the ground in many things. Do I have to live here?! I can think that I'm trapped inside this body, or I can think that it is the base to where I can always return. I need to use my limbs again; I have to be strong again! I have to eat more, and get less medicine!

Ah, I see that my thoughts are coming back! But which ones can I accomplish out of them? Which is exactly the one that I'm able to achieve, relying only on my deeds without external help? This is important. The biggest problem is the sedative. Somehow I need to stop them from giving it to me. I've already tried to talk with the nurses many times, but after the injection the one–sided communication always stopped, and after it I was just sleeping and sleeping. It has been going on for a long time. Now a lot of things are coming into my mind. Even the course I signed up for. I learned many techniques about using my brain and my words correctly. One thought! It seems that someone is calling, and looking for me. Ah, a fellow from the course! It has to be Agnes, who works in public health as a nurse. She was very distant when we met. She thought we had already met somewhere, on another planet. She remembers me. Her previous life was there, and this is the present one. She remembers clearly everything that happened to us. We were close friends. I can't remember this. My conscious doesn't show this to me. Maybe something bad happened to me there, which I haven't been able to reinterpret after so many times either. It's like me and motorcycling.

The motorcycle was the cause of my father's accident, and my previous death also. I hate motorcycles. Maybe I got phobia? But I love riding a bike! Feel the fresh air imbibing me, and takes away my negative thoughts. Like one of my friends in high school. He sat behind me. On one of the classes he cried out:

– Oh, my head hurts so much!

Everyone looked at him. The lesson continued. After the dismissal bell, he walked with a smile on his face towards the door of the room. Apparently, he was cheerful. I asked him on the corridor:

– What happened to you? You were very quiet!

– You know, I had a terrible head–ache! It was horrible! But after I said it out loud, I heard inside of me: this was only a breeze! It can be blown away also by a calm wind, I need nothing more! I closed my eyes. I concentrated strongly for several minutes. I gathered all the pain in my head to a single place; I put all the tiny parts into one place like a cleaning woman would do when she cleans up small glass particles. Systematically all in one place. A large ball formed in my mind, and I felt even more pain. I had to reduce this big ball to a size of a pea, and then to a size of a peppercorn. This also took a couple of minutes. In the meantime, my thoughts were always on the move. They were important too, but not as much as the pain in my head. I stretched my left arm aside, opened my palms, and concentrated on a strong wind that is going to come, and blow away my peppercorn–sized pain, which leaves me through my stretched arm with all its consequences. And guess what, it worked! This is the best! I am very happy! You are the first to whom I told this. Do you understand? I just had to think about it, and there's no pain in my body anymore! You know, it's so interesting for me to think about this. I imagined what could be inside someone's body, who is suffering from any kind of cancer. They can remove the unwanted pain from their body the same way, through their imagination! Is there anyone who managed to do it with a similar method? What do you think? – He asked.

– I don't know, but what you told me was very interesting. Related to this, another thing came into my mind, which happened at our home one summer, a few years ago. First the right, then the left side of my grandmother became paralyzed. I didn't know much of its details.

She lived in a small village on the countryside. The relatives discussed that after coming out of the hospital, she can spend the same amount of time at everybody's house for her to have better health provision. She could go four places, where she spent one month each. She arrived to us in the summer, in August, when it was very hot. She spent a lot of time in the garden. She was already seventy–seven years old, and after being in the hospital she needed a walking stick to walk safely. She really loved fruits. I concentrated many nights so that the nerves in her body could link, and be connected properly with each other. Through my stretched out palms I sent her imagined healing energy beams, and I was wishing that these healing energies would remove the breeze of her illness, and that all her energy paths should be cleared and free! She had to get rid of the limits, which were set by her many times, just to protect herself from some false fears.

Every night I sent her my imagined healing beams from the next room. In the morning, when she woke up, she was always looked for her walking stick to start her usual everyday work while leaning on it. After the third week she spent at our house she started to feel better. Probably, because she also wanted to recover. Once, she forgot her stick in the bathroom, and she was sitting on the bed in the room. When I saw her, I was very glad and asked her:

– Grandma, how many sticks do you have?

– Well, how many do you think I have? Only one, my son! Why?

– Because you forgot that only one in the bathroom, which means that you came here without it!

– Yes, yes! Please bring it to me! Thank you.

I brought it to her, and said:

– Grandma, you don't need a stick! It's just a habit that you have to have it in your hands! Leave it wherever you want, and walk, just as you're doing it now: without a stick!

We both laughed. She was getting better and better after this. She lived another ten years, even though the doctors gave her only a couple of years.

Agnes is looking for me telepathically, since she hasn't heard anything from me for a long time, and feels negative vibrations, as I hear. She is pushing her energy beams on me. She has always had strong energies, like the blown up Chernobyl nuclear power–station. It is nice that she is charging me. I feel her waves wishing me true recovery without any selfish will. The warmth overwhelms me. It's coming from her. It is like I am in the stomach of a volcano that is starting to erupt. But it's going to be too much! I need to cool myself down! Let's check my second chakra, my energy centre!

It is above the first one, and moves in the opposite direction as the one below. Its element: water, which slowly washes away everything in its way. This is what I need now. I can express my thoughts here, according to my present aims. I have to get out of here, recovered, and avoid another dose of medication. What shall I do? Should I be here or not? Can I pretend not to be here? I need to disappear from the sight of nurses, but I also need to stay here because I can't go out. They always close the doors, and the corridor is equipped with infrared sensors, as I can see this through the little window, standing right here at the door. Yes, I need to disappear; however, I must stay because of the food. I have to eat! I need strength, health! Yes, health. I have to meditate again. The four key elements are the most important.

EARTH, WATER, FIRE and AIR! Agnes is strongly giving her energies. I don't know how far she can be, but I hear that she knows that I'm full of drugs, and she's trying to clear them away from my body and veins with the power of fire. With fire, which always kills every disease. She is clearing me, I'm burning everywhere inside. I hope I will manage to stand it. I have to try to talk to the inner selves of the nurses, and keep a contact with them, or I have to ask my unconscious to restrict the sight of the nurses' by communicating with the parts of them that are outside their bodies. They shouldn't notice me in the room for several days. But before that I need to try it. I think I can count on Agnes, with her help my body will burn most parts of the harmful matters. The next time they come in, and bring my dose, I'm going to sit on the bed. I won't roll up the sleeve of my pyjama, but I will concentrate strongly so that they see it is, and they'll give me the injection. I may manage to tune in on their brainwaves. I also need to find the self in me, which is capable of doing all this with my other parts, together in harmony to reach a higher aim. Probably this part of me is much older than me, so I need even greater honour to approach it, and an even higher target should be pointed out to get out of here. Now it is not my life that counts. I have to think this through ...

If I manage to get out of here with their help, healthy and recovered, what will I do for my other fellow–beings? Anyway, is this part of me willing to be in contact with me? Or before I appear, shall I rephrase the chain of goals? Becoming stronger, eating, getting cleared from the drugs inside, being healthy, and perhaps temporarily being invisible for the nurses. We need a very long discussion here, inside! I need to talk honestly and respectfully with all my inner selves, without exceptions!

I'm locked. And what about other people who are living their everyday lives, are they locked up? What kind of walls did they build up around themselves? My walls are very close to me, but I have opportunities, and I may still have friends on the other side of the wall. There is no phone here, only telepathy, and my own inner resources. My body, which must be suitable for anything, if I clean it! Everyone has the same aim in me, we have already discussed this. Maybe only the circumstances independent from me can change things. I imagined pictures, and projected them into the future. Also the way I behave, feel, hear everything. And maybe the way that the nurses will respond. It was a big, life–sized, coloured picture with lifelike sounds. The events of several days, as if they had already passed by.

Projecting a volitional hallucination to someone else's brain can be the easiest, if I can accept the other person. If I'm able to understand his or her deeds, and through the deeds his or her aims. The nurses are elder, between forty and fifty years old. They must already have a family. I guess they have been working here for many years. They were envy about my tuition fee so possibly, they don't earn too well here. But still, they are here. They do their work fast and simple. The more the sedative is, the bigger the calmness is. I've never heard shouting here, neither any other sounds. I don't know through what kind of feedbacks they estimate the patients' current status. Maybe there are cameras inside the rooms. Ah, that's possible! I hear footsteps in the corridor. Somehow they know that I woke up, and I'm standing at the door! I can see through the small window that they're coming towards me. I see a sneering smile on their faces from far away. They have the same grin on their faces every day. I guess they really hate me, but I have to accept them and their aims as the way they are, otherwise neither of mine will come true. I sit down on the bed. Let's concentrate now! My left arm is stretched, my pyjama is not rolled up, but they have to think, it is. They are coming, the door is opening.

– Look, he has already got up, and wisely sat in position! – Says one of them.

– Very clever! By tomorrow he will have learn how to stand in attention as well!

– And I rolled up the sleeve of my shirt as well! You know, this is a very good sleeping sedative! I sleep very well from it, better than ever before! I could stand it all my life. Thanks for your care, guys! – And I'm stretching my arms toward them.

– Well, he is really crazy! What do you think?

– Do you want to stay here until the end of your life?

– Maybe – I answered

– This one is really crazy! I thought he's just an addict. Ok, put the food down for him, and I'll give him the injection!

His fellow went towards the table with a tray and put it down. I got my injection through my pyjama! I can't believe it, but it's in me. I managed to do it! I'm sleeping and sleeping again, while Agnes continues to burn me from the inside. She is destroying the illness in me with the help of the third chakra. My stomach started to boil. There's its place! I've already lived in this period from my fourteenth to my twenty–first. Fortunately this passed away, and after one year my life could enter the next one, the heart chakra. Here I accepted myself the way I am, and others as they are. I don't hate, and I don't like people, who are not nice to me, I just accept them. And if

I have a possibility to get to know them, I may form a positive opinion as well about a certain person.

If I didn't live in this chakra now, then my previous trick wouldn't work out either. I had to accept my "enemies" personality to get my sedative. I have already done the first step, now I need the burning! An urgent cleaning is needed in my body to get rid of the medicine. It's interesting; I hardly could wait for narcotics to absorb in me, and have effects over me. I absolutely didn't want to clear it from my body; what's more, I WANTED more! And now I want to be cleared from everything?!

I want to eat, I need help, and I should disappear for a few days. Perhaps my body's addiction to drugs has already stopped, but I miss the delirious pictures. What will call those beautiful pictures to my mind again which were so kind to me? The same dope again? That dope?! Am I hearing it well?

– I'll get you something else. You'll get new acquaintances, friends, if you get out of here. We will all help you from here, FOR YOU!

– Which part of me are you?

– One of them. I have also been neglected lately. I think that somehow you should address your other neglected selves with as much respect as you did with that very old one just now, who helped you to produce the nurses' hallucination! I have suggestions; listen to me, if you're interested! You know, and remember very well what you've heard about a lot of the people who recovered from various "diseases". Cancerous cells disappear from the body altogether with destructive thoughts. A man wearing a twenty dioptre eye–glass, and has astigmatism wants to read newspapers! After many decades of meticulous self–control, now he doesn't need any glasses anymore. Do you remember when you had a meeting in a hall of a hotel? You were dressed very elegantly: suit, tie, properly, as you should. You were going towards the café, when suddenly you saw the country's most famous fashion designer women coming towards you, who you have only seen before on television. She was coming towards you, you tried to avoid her, but she didn't allow it. She stopped, held her hand out, and introduced herself. You introduced yourself as well, then apologized and told her: you were glad to meet her, but you knew she was not waiting for you. She also apologized, and then had a look at her watch and said:

– It seems that whom I'm waiting for is late. But you know what, young man, the clothes can be different but the person is always the same.

You met someone you didn't expect; you can meet one of your selves the same way as well, somebody you're not even waiting for! And anyway can I ask something? Do you want to disappear? Do you think you can achieve with your nurses to stay invisible in this room for days, but they will bring you the food every day the same way as they did? You can make them hallucinate many things!

The first one is that you project into their minds that you're not physically here. Probably they begin to search for you, and then they'll analyze the images from cameras. They'll try to determine which way you escaped. They will call the security guard here, and then the police.

The other possibility is that you stay where you are. You don't disappear from their eyes, only or really leave them to give in your injections, or you achieve in their minds that they stick the prick next to your arm, and leave your dose to be poured on your bed for many days. That's how much time you need to get clean.

But you have also an opportunity to stop your breathing and life functions for a longer time, so that they legally declare your dead, and bury you. After this you can knock on your coffin from inside, under the ground, waiting for someone to open it. You may disappear for your family and friends forever, unless your parents ask for cremation, because in that case your body will disappear. If you are lucky, you can find a soul with a body lying in a coma somewhere in the astral world, and may get his body. However, if you go back to your parents in someone else's body, and you keep on asserting that you are their children, first you may get to the police station and later on, if you are lucky, you would get here again.

Take possibilities into account, all of them, which you can reach now with your present abilities. It's good if you know that you are not an Indian yogi, who tells his child to bury him in a coffin for about eighty years, then to mark the place, and leave it to his grandchild that he or she should be so kind to dig out your marked resting–place at a certain time, take off the lid, and wait for some days until you return to your body after the eighty–year–long transitory journey you made in the astral world, because you want to use your body again. Many times there are things you want to see in advance. Formerly, you just went into the so–called library of the future. You know, the past, the present and the future are all the same at a certain point, only the point of view should be chosen correctly. You read what happened later, and then you returned calmly to your body again from your night journey. Many people don't want to sleep a lot, they prefer to go out. To bars, casinos, etc. You like to spend a lot of time being in a sleeping position, lying, while you're flying here and there.

You are reading, you nosey boy!

Of course, I understand you. You are a Gemini, you are keen on flying, and information is everything for you. You would like to know what is going to happen tomorrow, but unfortunately the membership to the library of future expired when you started to use drugs. But you can get it again, if you want to! Note two things: first thing; give, give, give, and then once you will get it back. Thank it as much as you can! Then give, give, give! After this it will be the first time that you ask. Once, only once! You'll get it, but watch out, because we play in a team! Everything is connected to everything and everyone. The mob started the same way. After many things you gave, they get to know you, and by that time you can put in immodest claims, but gently! If you give them an inch, later on they will want to take a mile.

Do you know the joke? Three gangster frogs are talking on a shore. The first says: Croak. The second says: Croak. Finally the third: Croak–croak! The first frog shoots down the third. The second asks the third why he did. The answer: he knew too much!

You can't take somebody as such a fool, like you could be as well.

You should speak to the nurses' inner selves, with whom they probably aren't even in a nodding acquaintance, not even in their dreams. But YOU communicate with your inner parts quite well. Ask them to fulfill your request, and make the nurses give the injection next to your arm, because this way you are not drugged. If you get out from here recovered, they will have one patient less. You will pretend, you got the medicine. So you'll behave in the room like this. Apparently, you will lie on the bed dazed most of the day. Now you can only rely on your inner abilities, there's no help from outside! Many people, if they can, wait for external help to their problems. For example, overweight people or others who are suffering from any kind of health problems. Many people think that they go to doctors, non–medical practitioners, beauty salons. They pay and buy their health, buy their youth and beauty – or at least this is what they think. They buy illusions, and keep on pressing themselves with colourful, bright machines created by designers, or they simply sit in them. Health and beauty industries are about a lot of money. They make you buy your own dreams.

You get your illusion wrapped, which corresponds to the amount of your wealth. Although, everything is within you, you just have to take more care of yourself!

You have to put up some questions about drugs for yourself, but if you have the possibility, do it in deep hypnosis. The followings are essential:

Place and atmosphere. Where do you go regularly?

What do you do there? When you do what you do there regularly, what do you become capable of?

What does this mean to you? What is important in these skills?

What does it say about you? Who are you through this?

What is true about the world? What do you know about this? What is important in the world?

Who are you that these things are important to you? What is the important thing that you are over with that is even bigger than you?

At the University you wrote this on the inside your wardrobe: Slothfulness protects us from work, stupidity from knowledge! That's all I know. Work like a horse, every minute of the 24–hours can be used for idleness.

# Twenty–third Chapter

Now let's sit in a circle, everyone on their chair. Let's settle down in the most comfortable position. Close your eyes and breathe slowly, very slowly. As we breathe in the air more and more deeply, you may have noticed that all of us breathe rhythmically. Now I say the possibly simplest words to you slowly, very slowly so that everyone can understand them in the possibly best way. I always say the next word after exhalation, and since I speak very slowly, and we breathe the air in more and more slowly, therefore all parts of our bodies, from our toe tips to the top of our head, are relaxed the same way. Maybe we still have a few thoughts that are with us for a short time, but now we release them slowly, knowing that these are our thoughts as well, and we need them. We appreciate that they exist, and help us to solve our problems of life, but now, as they are moving away we take the direction to an even deeper state of consciousness in a complete rest, where our inner self is waiting upon us with full openness, and where we can meet the simplest ancient, pure love, in which all our deeds, what we have done till now, ease up as a drop in the ocean. Here we find the tranquility we have always looked for. Sometimes, maybe, when we are too busy, it would be worth it to immerse into this calm state, respecting the human nature that everyone learns in a different speed. We know that sometimes, in the future we are going to need such internal restful states, only for a few minutes to reassure our body in the rushing world around us.

We need to know that the deeper we are in ourselves, the deeper and more relaxed feeling it is for our entire being. In this state, even our internal organs can heal better, and positive changes, which have already started before, go on in a healthy direction.

Remember, what kind of inner power helped you regain your health. Perhaps now this power can be found in you even more, somewhere deep down in you, and is waiting for you to address it in a respectful manor, and ask from it everything that it has already done for you. For yourself.

This is a mighty power, which is able to stop the bleeding, if you hurt the skin on your finger, and to clean diseases and harmful cells from your body with the power of the burning fire. Always, in every moment even if you don't eat properly, this power sorts out the nutrients which can be used in the best way for your body, and removes the rest of it.

Maybe this part of you asked you a long time ago to eat healthier, and perhaps also asked you to work out more. Take his advice seriously, and get really necessary and healthy nutrients into your system. Perhaps by the intake of the outer materials into your system, you reached states that you believed temporarily to be important, but believe me, the most important thing is permanent health. Hallucinogenic substances can excite temporary good feelings, but in long term they are enemies, with whom you don't have to fight, it is enough, if you only leave them. Because you know very well that all the feelings in you are derived from you, so they are also born in you, not outside of you, so you can bring them out also from your inside.

The overflowing, long lasting happiness is associated with health, to what everyone is entitled. For you, for the people around you and all living creatures. Everyone has the right for a healthy life. So now we ask everyone, to work on this goal together, and let's empower ourselves that when this healthy life feeling is needed, whenever we want it, it should fully, with its biggest power, as fast as it can, be available for us. Anytime of the day, on winter, spring, summer, autumn and always.

Let's thank this power that it exists, and the fact that it will always help us as soon as possible. We need to know that we've found a mighty inner health source, which is always available for us, and there is only one thing that is even more powerful than this: the similar power that exists in all other human beings. If these powers sometimes join, they are able to help improve our fellow–beings edification on a long term. Our fellowmen, who are on the same vibe, can help us increase our power, this way we can do our everyday tasks faster and harder, with more energy. Thank this power that it is always and everywhere with you!

# Twenty–fourth Chapter

There are people who don't even have similar opportunities from their birth, let alone having skills. Many of them are born in a well–off, wealthy family, where all the goods are available. Their parents buy everything they can. These children are completely spoiled. Others are born with diseases in such families where almost everything is given for their recovery. They pre–select their future parents before their birth. Then, according to their possibilities, they have nine entire months to press all their knowledge acquired during their reincarnations with their own souls into their mother's placenta. This doesn't always happen absolutely well. Many children are born earlier with smaller mental deficiencies, bad sightedness, etc. This generally happens when the soul is unable to fully move into the body of the newborn. Some part of the soul stays behind in the great trip. This part remains in the astral world, and can't join. It's like when you download a program to your computer: If you interrupt the progress, the program won't run perfectly. Some people, even after many lives, just want to be a pretty girl, and enjoy life. Others, smart people who want to learn. They can gain several university diplomas. Everyone has other wishes. We bring along the legacy of our previous lives, while everyone experiences birth in a different way. It is very important for many people that the psychological trauma they may have suffered at birth becomes positive, since their further life can change only through this experience. It is possible that because of some reasons they live through the moment of birth as a trauma. This experience should be revaluated.

As the conditions of some people's birth are predicted, the moment of their death can also be. Everything is in one single point: the past, the present, and the future. If we want to see them, we must enrol in the appropriate school. We need to find the appropriate position to observe this point the most effective way, and by altering this position we can turn the pages in the great book. What do we want to see? We need to stand there! Unfortunately, the future is the way it should be! What the Bible says can be interpreted, but we can have a look on our present lifestyle as well. There are things that not even our grandchildren will see. But they WILL see high garbage hills! Who will be the true ones, who can survive everything? Those who survive a global nuclear attack, and can wait for its end in a specially constructed nuclear bunker, and are able to wait several years, maybe until the Earth and its atmosphere become clean?

Will the water and the earth become clean? Will the ionizing radiation disappear from them? Once I met a chemical engineer who confessed the dualism: Yin and Yang. We began to talk about similar topics. He made experiments with destroying nuclear waste radiating materials, and the results were extremely surprising. He prepared a mixture of different materials, which interacted with emitting particles of fuels removed from nuclear power plants, and broke them into dust; in addition the radiation effects are completely eliminated. The gentleman visited several agencies as well. The answer, he got, was simple: they'd rather build nuclear waste storages, because in long–term there is more money in that, than the protection of people's health.

During the time of their current position, officers are motivated to load their pockets with money! Part of humanity can decide what is good for others. Is it all right that a small part of all, load their pockets at the price of other's health?

What would happen in a nuclear war? How many souls would leave their body there? Where could they be born? Lots of murderers kill, or have someone killed because they think that the person believed to be annoying or hostile will disappear from their material life.

Yes, the soul flies away from the body, which keeps it moving. But the "astral police" are terrible, their mental strength, with which they are able to affect souls of people moving on earth, and to punish their so–called conscience. Police? Yes they are.

They are irreproachable, have clear morals, and they can't be bribed! If you do anything bad in your material life, and if it is possible to adjust it, you will get a chance to turn it good. In severe cases you are sentenced to prison. You are locked up, and you can wait somewhere regressed, for a long time the day of your rebirth.

You can be a handicapped child in a healthy family where parents have no other desire but to see you healthy. You are punished until you learn. Life is cruel, and absolutely fair. Everyone gets the fruits or curses of his or her deeds! You can arrive to a healthy family, maybe to normal parents, who may wonder decades later, what has become of their child. They couldn't imagine this! You don't even resemble to the character of your parents, but even with the relatives there is only a little similarity. Even your eyes don't look like anyone else's in the family. And your behaviour is completely different then what they would of expected from you. You do exactly the opposite, as you should. Many people talk about the contrast between generations. Or, it is all about your selfish interests and needs to be fulfilled, so you had the opportunity to choose your future parents. They expected something completely different from you.

You feel good in whatever you do. You are not interested in their opinion now or later on. Perhaps you will be a parent once as well, and you don't know the character of your future child. As no one knows it beforehand exactly. A long time ago there was a very significant tradition to forecast the birth of the future child. Before and during the birth highly competent experts were praying for days to the soul of the unborn child, so that everything will be perfect at the moment of the arrival.

Nowadays, in a usual labour ward, only doctors and nurses are present to help a living body be born. They often don't really care about the soul itself. They assist at several births, and then the ones after that. It's a routine. There was a small complication here. Maybe from difficult cases, educational materials will be presented in the professor's collection.

Every birth is worth a new aim. A soul gets a new opportunity to develop further in a body. The goal is to improve its unconscious. Many times the conscious self doesn't perceive many things, but our unconscious part helps us in this several times. For example, when you can't find something, then you ask yourself, and suddenly it comes into your mind where you put the house key.

Someone inside of you tells you. Our inner part, who wants to help us with this as well. Because we are in the same team with them. Other times two completely contradictory opinions are expressed in us, when we would like to go somewhere with someone just as much as we do not. In this case, two or more of our inner parts consider different aspects, probably to achieve their goals for their, and for our own interests. In several cases like this, it is possible that not the decision is the point, but our own internal dialogues, and the process and strategy of it. Many times we can think of a certain everyday series of action as a chain reaction. It can also become a habit to think about things always in the same order. However, if we notice in our inner self the condition that brings this state, and the chain reaction of the thoughts, even by watching the chain of thoughts from the outside, then we can see these permanent characteristics in ourselves, thus we can get to know the pattern of our own thinking.

These also tend to be influenced by the conditions derived from our upbringing, and the experiences followed by them. If you think that you want to alter a certain act, then in the beginning it is enough to change your thinking scheme at one point, and later on the whole chain is able to transform in a better direction for you. It can be interesting when you look on yourself from outside, or project yourself in other people's places.

This way, in our imagination we can determine our own path and line of life. It is enough if we think about an absolutely neutral, everyday activity which doesn't generate either negative nor positive thoughts or feelings in us. Let's have a look, how did we do it ten years ago. How do we do it now? And how will we do the same thing one year, and ten years later?

If all our pictures are pretty, and we see them clearly as well as their position in space around us, we can link them together with a fictive line. Thus we can get our Lifeline on which we can put our future acts, but we can go back on it in the past to get positive experiences, and powers which can steady ourselves by bringing them into the present. We can go back and forth on this as far as our unconscious allows it.

We can even go back before the date of our birth. We can be born again and again. In the beginning we are a tiny cell. Later on we were a plant, then a multitude of animals, and in the end human. A Human who waits for enlightenment, eternity. Who tries to become one with things by considering them. This is a long road, where we don't tolerate big differences that are unknown for us, the things that come from the outer world, but by being annoyed by them we become angry instead of asking ourselves: what does this human want to teach me? Why am I angry now? What is the thing that I can't accept in this situation? What could be his or her positive aim?

At the beginning many questions remain unanswered in us, which later on can make sense in their own reality together by being cleared, with its entire context.

We would like to extend our inner part as a whole, with the fact that after a certain age we look for a partner from the other sex. Of course, there are exceptions as well, but everyone tries to find, searches for his or her other half, although there are some people who never find it.

That inner unit, which evolves within the Human, respects its inner parts, their aims, the animals living figuratively in our body, and their symbols, the inner "gods". We should become one with these things through our inner and outer relationships, by forming and improving them.

Improving opinions could be perceived as criticism. But our common, highest aim is always the same for everyone, regarding animals and plants as well. Happiness, light, nirvana, eternal life, etc.

There are many words to describe the last phase of human existence in the body before death. The spirit, whether it is prepared to enlighten (not the best word), tolerate and accept, it is able to integrate everything and everyone with all the good and bad characteristics and it is also able to accept that duality that with the movement of things, it goes through a continuous, unstoppable development in all areas of life. When I imagine myself as an iron ball, or as a piece of firewood burning in a fireplace and I long for earthly existence, the four elements, and eternity, well, then I have to admit that, yes, this will eventually be given to everyone, but till then, many rebirths will happen in several random shapes.

The basic essence of the four elements is the aether, in which, after the last earthly life, the human will dissolve, as sugar in hot tea. But then this energy streams through the endless sea of time. From the aether some kind of material evolves, from which a living creature, an animal, then a human or a human–like creature is formed again. Later on it develops into a basic material again and then again and again to aether.

Our little lives are like tony marbles on a huge desk, where a huge and incomprehensible someone considers our existence, and decides our fate. When does it want to play with which ball? "He" lives in a huge castle with a very large garden on an area of thousands of billion hectares. Perhaps we are even smaller than an ant for him. Planets disappear, and new ones are formed. We, people, are talking about billions of years but for him these are only tenth of seconds.

Everyone believes in something, usually in those things that are personally experienced. We trust better in these things. But there are several things that can't be accepted by everyone. Perhaps the distance may seem new that some measure it in light–years, while others measure it in astral seconds. The journey can be done in many ways. With a person you can talk several ways. You can look for your own selfish interests in a short distance, or you can help in the long run. WHAT is the aim? And what is the higher aim? When I reach it, then what is the goal, of which no higher one exists?

Eternal life? Do not worry! For your soul another chain of lives start from the beginning, always in a higher level.

And what should I do now? Where do I live? Do I have needs? Can I satisfy them? Can I bring joy to others?

# Twenty-fifth Chapter

What will the future be like? Controlled life, GPS, and location detecting systems implanted in dogs, retina and fingerprint readers? Isolated areas for certain parts of humanity? Social networks and other forms of discrimination? Sectors and human communities separated from each other? Tracking and access control systems? Will the portable water purification device become a human value? Who will be the real human? The one who can distinguish a lie from the truth, or the one who notices the iniquity in others?

In a World War II movie defeated German troops were coming home for from Russia. They walked in big snow at wintertime, chilled to the marrow with little food. On the way some of them noticed a smaller group. Russian people were sitting with blankets rolled around them, at the edge of the snow–filled road in minus twenty – thirty degrees. They reached out with their hands, asking for food or drink from the soldiers of the retreating enemy. But they weren't actually enemies, but the very cold, and the pangs of hunger which affected everyone. A German soldier stopped, his fellows went on, and then a few moments later they stopped, and looked back to their friend, who reached into his frozen jacket, and put a piece of bread on one of Russian's outstretched hands. He thanked it with a nod, and put it into a woman's hand lying behind him. She folded back a blanket, and tried to force the bread into a toddler's mouth with her hands, the bit which meant survival for the one–and–a–half year old baby.

We can only rest in peace if we were able to arrange all of our tasks and human relationships to everyone's satisfaction. Can I give something to my environment from myself, which helps their improvement to be better? I must continue to do so while I live! I have to do so in harmony with all living beings that I work on them being better. The rest will be solved by time instead of me.

I am very frightened of the moment when my parents leave me here. I think of them every day very hard, but when they will die, I have to be able to let them go with all my thoughts about them.

It's going to be difficult. I have to continuously arrange my human and astral relationships.

14421986R00083

Made in the USA
Lexington, KY
28 March 2012